native american magic

essentials

native american magic

essentials

james lynn page

foulsham

LONDON • NEW YORK • TORONTO • SYDNEY

foulsham

The Publishing House, Bennetts Close, Cippenham, Slough,
Berkshire, SL1 5AP, England

ISBN 0-572-02740-0

Cover illustration by Jurgen Ziewe

Printed in England by Cox & Wyman Ltd, Reading, Berkshire

Contents

The Native American Today – Keeping the Flame Alive

In the early 1990s, a British travel writer was invited to a Native American reservation to witness a gathering of performing dancers. The traditional dance was in honour of the Spirit, the great being, the grandfather, the mysterious source of all life. Visitors from another reservation some 60 kilometres (40 miles) away arrived to participate in the spirit dance and found a generous collection of gifts awaiting them. Among these were the traditional ceremonial blankets, though in this case made of nylon. Then the elder rose to offer a welcoming speech in a regional tribal language known as Lushootseed. An attempt was being made at the time to keep the language alive, with the aid of a university anthropologist, and the offer of night-school classes to the local people. Soon, the dance began. A piercing shriek cut the air as a shaman rose to his feet and began to intone a song to the Spirit. As his body writhed and shook furiously, others joined in, using the shamanic ritual instruments, drums and rattles, to emphasise the steady rhythmic pulse.

The travel writer watching was left largely unimpressed, just as previous Western witnesses to the spirit dance (as far back as 200 years previously) had been. Their verdict on this curious sight ranged from 'a series of spasmodic jumps' and 'jumping in a very peculiar manner' to 'simply a jumping up and down'. The outward image however is not the real point: it is merely a method, a very powerful one in fact, of transcending normal, everyday consciousness and becoming aware of the Spirit. What is most poignant here is that the traditional war-like dance no longer serves a practical purpose. In the earlier days of hunting on the plains for buffalo, such dances were used in a ritual, or magical, way to attract the animal. The travel writer came away with the impression of little more than an elaborate entertainment. Having witnessed the spirit dance, he was about

to call in at the local casino and play the roulette wheel. The Native American embrace of certain areas of modern culture made for an incongruous mix. It all seemed such a far cry from the days of the vision quest, night after night in a wilderness fraught with danger, lying beneath the stars, with neither food nor shelter, to partake of one's first initiation into the Spirit.

In spite of these changes, the modern struggle to retain the early teachings goes on. Depending on your opinion, the often downgraded lifestyle of modern Native Americans is either an unfortunate result of history (and the triumph of the 'White Man') or an unnecessary tragedy in which a people's traditional culture has been all but eroded. Ever since the Native Americans were herded into reservations in the late nineteenth century, like so many cattle, it was the beginning of the end for the old ways. The patronising attitude towards the Indian (Native American) at that time is best summed up in the words of cleric George Ellis in 1882: 'The Indian must be made to feel he is in the grasp of a superior'.

Of course attitudes have changed radically since then. There are still critics who say that America doesn't do enough to help its indigenous people, but there is now plenty happening in modern America whereby traditional Amerindian culture can thrive. Whether this is the weekly pow wow, churches erected to worship the Amerindian religion, or art and craft pursuits like spirit paintings and beadwork, there is now a strong move to maintain the traditional teachings, and this is crucially important because this is a culture that reveres the past with intense passion, whose racial memory of its roots could never truly be eroded. In any case, to talk of keeping the Spirit alive would be seen as arrant nonsense by the medicine man of today, for as we shall see later in this book, the Spirit, in a very real sense, can never die.

Some of the ideas and philosophies covered in this book may seem rather unfamiliar to the modern reader, what with descriptions of medicine wheels, totem beasts and magical invocations of the Great Spirit. In the Western world, we live in a material environment that resists most of our attempts to influence it by anything other than sheer will power, and it can seem to us that the physical world we inhabit is nothing other than a series of disconnected objects. Even our own experiences, through our five senses, make it feel as if our personal universe is limited to the boundaries of our own body. To Native Americans, however, looking out upon a ruby sunset, or watching the eagle swooping down on its prey, all these visual sensations do not merely occur externally, they are part of a continuum that links with their own internal being. This may be difficult for us to understand; we have been taught to believe that the world we observe has no real relationship to the observer. But Native Americans do not draw this distinction between inner and outer worlds, indeed they feel intimately at one with both. This may sound too mystical to Western thinking, although it can be shown that this sense of oneness –

far from being some airy-fairy spiritual delusion – is, in fact, an enlightened view of reality.

It is one thing to say that one feels part of the environment or at one with Nature, but what does it mean to experience it in a religious sense? What exactly do we mean when we use these phrases? Everything that happens to us is ultimately the experience of our mind (conscious and subconscious), as the world appears to come to us via the senses. There is the 'I' that experiences and the external world that is experienced, and yet it is possible, in a very real way, to see beyond this division and feel that all is one. This is the main goal of Native American magic, since real inner harmony, wholeness, leads naturally to being in proper relationship to the rest of the world. Here, there are parallels to some of the work of psychologist Carl G. Jung, whose ideas about psychic integration and the necessity for coming to terms with the total Self are in turn mirrored by Eastern wisdom like Taoism and Zen. But let's return to our

Amerindians (inner), gazing on their red sunset (outer). It is just as true to say that the eyes see redness due to the setting sun, as it is to say the sun is red because of our eyes. Our perceptions of the world are often far more subtle and complex than we realise.

The aim of Native American magic is to attune oneself to the Great Spirit, and to keep that relationship alive. The meditation and visualisation exercises that appear in the final chapters of this book are designed to provide the modern reader with access to the Spirit. I shall attempt to show that the Spirit, far from being merely a mystical idea, is an unacknowledged reality behind reality. In one sense, the real world is an illusion, in that the forms it assumes are never the final reality. Its true substance is spiritual, a field of vibrational patterns with their own hidden power. Indeed modern science acknowledges that all matter is actually a slow vibration of energy. Even humans are made of this field of force, this energy. And so, since everything is made of it, it must be everywhere. Science also says that energy cannot be destroyed, only transformed. Here, then, is the truth that Amerindian teachers have known intuitively for many years. Apache shaman Ernesto Alvarado says: 'When we die ... the energy's going to change. But it's going to go on 'cos it's the Life Force. We came from there ... It's in the shell [but] the shell is not me. The shell doesn't define me. It just holds me together for now.' This is the deeply spiritual, deeply humble, but life-affirming attitude behind Native American teaching.

Chapter 1
We are Part of the Earth

The Mayflower pilgrims, who set sail for the New World in 1620, were supposedly learned and sophisticated Westerners. They were, however, almost wiped out because they were hopeless at finding sufficient food to eat – even in a land of abundant food supplies, with birds and deer to be hunted, wild fruits to be gathered and fish to catch. The local so-called savages, the Wampanoag tribe, saved them from dying of malnutrition. Squanto, an Indian who could speak English, instructed them in the arts of hunting and of planting corn seed, enabling the settlers to thrive. The pilgrims had found a people highly adept at living off the land, highly skilled game hunters, with an innate intuition about successful crop growing. Squanto had no reason to feel charitable towards these bumbling settlers. Fifteen years earlier he had been kidnapped and sold into slavery. When he finally returned to his homeland he found that his tribe had been devastated by smallpox, almost certainly contracted from foreign explorers.

The fact that Squanto befriended the white settlers epitomises much about the Native American attitude to their homeland. They did not insist that the new settlers stay off the land, but instead offered to share it with them. The environment for them is a living entity to be respected, and the concept of owning a piece of land is quite alien to them. They see themselves in the role of caretaker for successive generations, and far from it being their land, the surrounding environment has been provided for their use and care. This concept derives from their deeply spiritual beliefs concerning the Great Spirit, the mysterious source of creation that informs all Native American philosophies. The Great Spirit is believed

to have created both the land and the Amerindian. The Amerindians therefore identify with the land as just as much a part of the natural environment as the trees, streams, wind and sky. They are not merely living off the land, they are related to it; the wild animals are their brothers; their mother is the earth.

A Cancerian People

The Amerindians differ greatly from modern Westerners in one very powerful respect. It is in this sense of belonging to something greater; their environment gives them a sense of identity so powerful that to remove them from their homeland would be to take away a piece of their soul. The idea of conquest of the land, the taming of Nature, does not fit in with their beliefs. For the wilderness beyond the tipi is also where they live. This sense of being at home wherever they may find themselves is beautifully demonstrated in the anecdote about a hunting guide out one day with a white colleague. When it appeared that they had lost their direction home, the white man commented smugly, 'You're lost, Chief!'. Unembarrassed, the Indian replied, 'Indian not lost. Tipi lost'.

For those readers acquainted with astrology, there is a fascinating cosmic coincidence in that the traditional birth chart for modern America (dated either 2 or 4 July 1776) has Cancer as its sun sign. Though the Amerindian tribes had, of course, already inhabited North America for hundreds of years before the eighteenth century, the characteristics of this sign are to a large extent embodied in these original natives. Cancer relates to family, mother, roots, the past, the home, feminine intuition and the imagination. The important element is belonging to a family or home, having an awareness of where you come from, and a sense of security and continuity with the past.

These qualities also apply to the Amerindian peoples with their deep love of and respect for family and ancestors, as is seen in the clan system. Their sense of the past is represented, for example, in the carved totem poles of the north-west coast tribes. These were used as front panels outside their homes and illustrated the history of the clan. Being a Cancerian people, the importance of women's role in clan society should not be underestimated. Males from the Navajo tribe, for example, joined their wife's family when they married, bringing with them their wealth and resources. Cancer is a sign of nurture, and appropriately, the Native American family is an extremely close-knit unit where care for both old and young is taken for granted. We have seen the fragmentation of the family unit in our modern world, with both parents often in full-time occupations. The Amerindian would find the notion of a child-minder or an old people's home detestable. As Sun Bear, a Chippewa medicine chief remarks, 'even today, the Indians don't leave their children home with a babysitter when a pow wow comes up'. And so it has always been.

Before the 'White Man'

Amerindians are extraordinarily proficient at adapting to their natural environment. Tribes living near the sea developed maritime and fishing skills, using birch bark canoes and spears. Those living on the plains hunted buffalo, not simply for meat, but for all its resources. The skins would be used for house exteriors or footwear whilst the sinews provided thread for sewing clothes. The bones could be fashioned into tools for leather working, and even the dung would be dried out and used as fuel for the fire. Some of these Amerindians – the Apaches of the Texas Panhandle for example – were nomadic, following around the buffalo herds, and living largely off the resources they provided. Other communities were more settled and lived in villages. Here they built houses from wooden frames, using trees from the nearby forests. The frames were then draped with mats or tree bark and secured with straw and mud. Apart from gathering wild fruits and nuts, and occasionally hunting deer, the most important food supply for the inland, settled tribes was corn. In fact, it was corn that saved the lives of the Mayflower settlers. The Apache Geronimo sums up this feeling of a beneficent Great Spirit that provides for all of his needs: 'He' had created a home for each tribe, and there 'He placed whatever would be best for the welfare of the tribe'.

All this may paint rather an idyllic picture, but survival for the Amerindian hunters was not something that was taken for granted, and they had to develop the necessary fitness and physical stamina to cope with their way of life. The plains tribes required runners, for example, to go ahead and seek out suitable places in which to camp. They might also have to cover up to 80 kilometres (50 miles) a day in pursuit of elk or deer, sometimes lying in wait by the prey's watering place for a full day. Alternatively, they might rub dried sage over their bodies to prevent the game scenting them, then silently stalk their quarry. Having caught their prey, they would dry out the meat under the sun and cut it into thin slices, then grind it. The nomadic tribes (such as the Blackfoot and Cheyenne) then stored the dry mash to be used later in cooking, once settled elsewhere. Fish, on the other hand, was cooked as soon as it

was caught. It could be wrapped in clay and then baked, or placed in a dugout, covered with leaves and then roasted over hot coals.

The Amerindians are in tune with Nature. They rely upon and trust in the Great Unseen as their provider. The entire land is alive with spirits, which are joined with the Amerindians' own, and at the centre is this mysterious Spirit. The changing rhythms of Nature, both seasonal and daily, are also the Amerindians' nature, their unbreakable union with the world. In the words of Chief Seattle, a nineteenth-century head of the Duwamish people: 'Man has not woven the thread of life' for 'whatever he does to the web, he does to himself'. The emphasis is not only on ecological concerns (for Amerindians are born conservationists) but with the spiritual principles behind their existence. You may argue that the plains tribes kill the buffalo, who is their brother, but this is their only food source, and the killing is therefore necessary for survival. In any case, they would offer a prayer prior to the hunt and perform the buffalo dance in its honour. A far cry from the later white settlers who, at one time, took up shooting buffalo as a kind of casual sport. And so, 'the fragrant flowers are our sisters, the reindeer, the horse, the great eagle our brothers' says Chief Seattle. 'The foamy crests of waves in the river, the sap of meadow flowers, the pony's sweat and the man's sweat is all one and the same race, our race.'

This sense of beauty, sensitivity and feeling for the poetic can be seen in various place names of Indian origin: Mississippi, Saskatchewan and Susquehanna. Even more arresting are the various tribal terms: Shuswap, Nootka, Onondaga, Shoshonean, Athapascan. Then of course there are the many individual names, often startling to European ears. Some derive from totem animals associated with a particular tribe, such as Crazy Horse, Sitting Bull, Sun Bear or Lame Deer, or perhaps from personal qualities and abilities. The nineteenth-century warrior Cochise was named for his steadfastness and loyalty since his name means 'like ironwood'. Others were given names like Ba-da-ah-chon-du, meaning 'he who outjumps all', or Niganithat, 'he who flies first', a member of the Kickapoo tribe. Then there is the Nez Perce tribe, among whose members were Rabbit Skin Leggings and No Horns on his Head. Whatever their language, tribal customs or geographical location, the

Amerindian people were united in their common, mystical feel for the homeland and their oneness with Nature.

The Native American people make sense of life through the heart and the emotions. The world, in all its forms and movement, communicates with them in a very real sense, since the Great Unseen Spirit is everywhere. The flight of the eagle, the bubbling streams and boiling sea, the majesty of the landscape with its mountain peaks or endless vistas, all of this contains a rich poetry and beauty for the Amerindian. The forms of Nature – an oddly shaped rock, cloud formation or waterway – are full of symbolism and meaning. In these ways, the Great Unseen is speaking to them. Thus one of the very earliest descriptions on record from a foreign explorer on an expedition in 1541 describes the Amerindians as, 'a gentle people, not cruel … and skilled in the use of signs'. Ever since Columbus reported back that there was a placid race of people living in a bountiful New World, explorers have sought to conquer and colonise. But the explorers would find them a little less gentle this time.

After the 'White Man'

The first attempts by Westerners to colonise the New World date back to the early sixteenth century. Most were Spanish explorers who found the natives helpful and accommodating. The Native Americans were usually prepared to share their food and provide guides for exploration. When the settlers pressed their demands too far, however, Amerindian patience became stretched and hospitality began to evaporate. By the late 1500s, many more Spaniards were entering America via its south-west coast (they already had a slight hold on Florida) and in 1595 Spain decided on a firm policy of colonisation. By the time of the first English settlers in 1607 (13 years before the *Mayflower*), the Amerindians had good reason to be suspicious, and the arrival of George Percy and company in Virginia, for instance, was greeted by a hail of arrows. The following 300 years saw wars between the Western settlers and the indigenous peoples as the Amerindians struggled for survival and to retain their beloved homeland. At the same time, of course, the War of Independence was being fought. Once England relinquished

its power over the former colony, the new enemy of the Amerindian peoples was no longer marauding invaders but people who called the same land their home.

The new, white inhabitants of North America encroached further on to the Amerindians' sacred territory. By 1886, at the end of the last Amerindian wars, various areas were earmarked for the Native Americans, who were shunted into reservations; and they hated them. As one commentator justified it, 'as long as Indians live in villages they will retain many of their old and injurious habits ... heathen ceremonies and dancing'. The Amerindian peoples were contained on the reservations in order to 'begin their real and permanent progress'. They were to be turned into an inferior version of the new settlers. This arrogance on the part of 'superior' colonists was evident from the start, when one of the reasons for Columbus's voyage had been to convert the 'heathen' to Christianity. For the Sioux and the Cheyenne, in particular, the proud and impassioned nomadic hunters of the wild plains, the reservation meant life-sapping boredom. Nothing could be more hurtful to the Amerindian spirit, to a people accustomed to freedom in the landscape that was once their home.

It is no surprise that the Amerindians, as Cancerians, were prepared to fight so fiercely for their homeland. They were trying to safeguard a part of their soul. Forcing them to leave their home was like breaking their heart. As Geronimo once put it, 'when they are taken from these homes they sicken and die'.

An old Yuma Indian expresses this sentiment ever more succinctly when he says to the 'White Man', 'Yes, we know that when you come, we die'. He wasn't simply referring to the battlefield either, but rather to the sickness of heart and spirit that would result when the Amerindians were torn from their roots. And so the Native American learned to fight.

Just as they could live skilfully off the land, so they developed cunning tactics in warfare. The Spanish introduced horses to the New World and, in time, they were appropriated by the Comanches of the southern plains. From then on, the horse would be indispensable to the Sioux, the Nez Perce and the

Cheyenne in their battles for freedom. The Cheyenne rope, for example, was a sling placed over the body of the horse, that enabled the rider to get a single foothold as he crouched down on one side of the animal, making himself invisible to an unsuspecting enemy. The Amerindian even drew praise from an American Lieutenant after the Battle of Little Bighorn, 'they were all keen, athletic young men, tall and lean and brave … perfectly adapted to the environment, and knew just what to do in every emergency'.

But the Amerindians' skills could not save them from defeat in war with the 'White Man'. Defeat is perhaps not the right word, however, as the Amerindian does not believe in death! The spirits of the ancestors live on, inhabiting anything from rocks and trees to the whispering breeze. The land on which the Amerindians live and the air that they breathe are impregnated with the spirits of the dead. Just as the sign Cancer likes to keep the past alive, so the Amerindians revere that which has gone before. This is not mere sentimentality for days long gone, either, for the sense of eternal spirit, tradition and knowledge which comes from the past and moves on into the present lies at the roots of Native American belief and magic. Think of the medicine man's psychic communion with a dead relative, who passes on wisdom from beyond the grave. To the cynic, this is mere fancy, but perhaps we should all remember that what we are taught to believe from an early age has a far more powerful effect on our life than we might admit. Belief is a powerful force in magic; it is what makes the magic happen. There is also much documented evidence from sceptical observers, who are unable to pass off the Native American medicine man's magic as mere fakery. As well as enriching our culinary habits and vocabulary, the Amerindians have given us a great legacy in their spiritual tradition of magic and storytelling. At least nowadays, the Amerindian brave has no more need to declare on the battlefield: 'it's a good day to die'. But then, in the words of Chief Seattle: 'Death – I say? There is no death. Only a change of worlds.'

Chapter 2
Native American tales

In the beginning there was a vast, unchanging watery expanse, over which two doves flew. Eventually, this expanse formed into mud, and a single, lonely blade of grass could be seen poking through the slime. In time, a hill appeared, and this was the home of the god Esaugetuh Emissee, whose name means 'Master of Breath'. From the muddy clay that surrounded his home, he fashioned the first people. However, since much of the earth was still flooded with water, he had to construct a huge wall on which to dry his creations. In time, the clay from which people were formed would turn into hardened bone, covered in flesh. Esaugetuh then ensured that the vast waters were separated from the dry land. Thus did mankind appear on the earth – according to the Muskhogeans, an ethnic division of the Amerindian peoples from the area we would now call the Deep South.

In the Algonquian version, their great deity Michabo was out hunting with his wolves when he noticed something curious: the animals ahead of him were entering a huge lake and promptly disappearing beneath the water. He was about to follow and rescue them, when the lake swelled and overflowed until it covered the entire land. Undaunted, the god sent forth

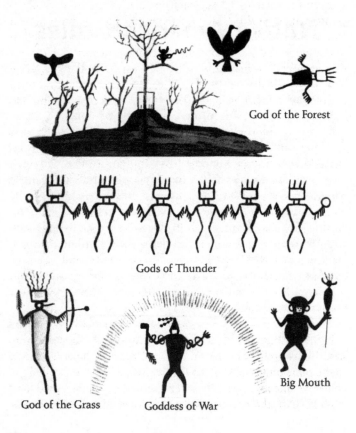

God of the Forest

Gods of Thunder

God of the Grass

Goddess of War

Big Mouth

a raven in order to find a patch of dry earth from which to create a new world. Unfortunately, the bird was unsuccessful and so the god sent an otter to do the same, but it too failed to find a piece of dry land. Finally, Michabo sent forth a musk-rat that eventually returned with enough earth for the god to be able to create a dry new world. Michabo and the musk-rat were then joined in marriage, and their offspring became the human race.

These are two of the many richly imaginative legends that arise out of Amerindian culture. They have strong similarities with stories from the Bible, in particular Genesis 2:6–7, which tells of an earth covered with water and how God made mankind from the dust of the ground. Later a raven is sent by Noah from the ark to discover whether there is anywhere on earth where the flood has subsided. Whilst the similarities with the Amerindian creation myths have been attributed to the influence of early Christian missionaries, no such link needs to be made. Ancient cultures, in fact, developed their myths and folk legends independently of one another, as has been shown by psychologist Carl Jung, among others. Diverse cultures all have their sun god, mother goddess, weather deity or a divine being presiding over success in love, war or the harvest. Jung saw this as proof that the human race plugs in, unconsciously, to the same universal source. This source, which Jung called the collective unconscious, is best represented by a submerged land mass beneath the ocean. Whilst individual islands (societies or individuals) above the water line appear to be separate, they are all connected beneath. Jung saw this as the reason for the patterns and memories that are common to all humanity. The stories appear similar because we are all subject to the same hopes, fears, dreams, fantasies, and often codes of behaviour. Of course, as certain cultures develop technologically and intellectually, such tales of monsters, demons, sea nymphs and fantastical gods are demoted to the realm of the children's story book. Amerindian legends, however, have always taken a far more important place in their culture, well into the era of so-called civilisation. The Amerindians view events that are beyond their control as the handiwork of the gods. The Westerner sees this as too simple a way of explaining things. For the seagoing tribes on America's north-west coast, for example, the terror of the deep, its whirlpools and threats from killer whales and octopuses were manifestations of Komogwa, the Wealthy One, the Master of the Sea who dwelt below in his sub-aquatic palace. And so, as late as 1868, we find the Amerindian world view described as, 'the meaningless play of capricious ghosts. He investigates not, because he doubts not. All events are to him miracles.'

The Pipe of Peace

For the Native American, the fantastic and the ordinary, the miraculous and mundane are to be found everywhere, and in the same place. The tale of how the peace pipe came to the

Amerindians is a good example of this. Many years ago the Great Spirit called upon his people from the Red Pipe-stone Quarry. He took a chunk of stone from the wall and fashioned it into a massive pipe, which he proceeded to smoke, emitting fumes to all four directions of the compass. He told his people that this red stone was the same as their own bodies, their flesh, and that from the rock they should make peace pipes. (In another version, since the Great Spirit was addressing different tribes who had been at war with one another, the red rock came from the ground on which the blood of the slain had been spilt.) The message was that Amerindian must no longer fight Amerindian. Hostility was to be banished by smoking the pipe of peace. When the Great Spirit had spoken to his people, he disappeared in a cloud, leaving behind a glazed surface on the rock.

The sacred place mentioned above does actually exist –
presumably nearby the place named Pipestone, Minnesota. It is
described by Victorian traveller George Catlin as 'truly an
anomaly in nature', being a massive 'perpendicular wall of close
grained, compact quartz, of twenty five and thirty feet in
elevation' which runs to about 'two miles in length'. For many
centuries, Native Americans came to this place to obtain the red
stone. Smoking the peace pipe is more than mere recreation,
rather it is a ceremony to honour the wishes of the Great Spirit,
to take in some of his breath. Of course, in the words of a
Victorian commentator it is 'nothing more than a tobacco pipe,
splendidly adorned with savage trappings', though admittedly,
'a sacred thing to be used on only the most solemn occasions'.
In the words of one modern medicine man, the pipe is like, 'an
open Bible'. It is, for him, a method for receiving the power of
Wakan Tanka (the Sioux phrase for Great Spirit, Great
Mystery). 'Power flows down to us through that smoke ... the
pipe is not just a thing, it is alive.'

Totems

The word totem comes from the tribal language of the
Algonquian-Ojibwa people from around the Great Lakes area.
Absorbed into the English language in the late eighteenth
century, it has come to mean a kind of guardian from whom the
Amerindians would receive instruction – a helper whose
strength and protection offers support in times of trial. Yet the

original sense of the word suggests a more intimate relationship with the Amerindians: for the word *ototeman* formerly meant 'his brother-sister kin'.

To the Native Americans, Nature is alive with meaning, symbolism and, more importantly, the powers of communication. There is no real difference between animate Nature (birds in flight, the animals of the forest) and the inanimate (rocks, hills, trees, the earth). Since the Spirit is present in all of creation, then the world around the Amerindians must contain the intelligence of that Spirit; it is, in fact, conscious. A tree rustling in the night may be whispering with the voice of one's ancestors; the wind, as it howls beyond the tipi, may be issuing a warning of danger ahead in the next valley; and the gushing rivers or seas, in their fathomless depth and the shapes they create, may be predicting the future. This belief that everything in Nature contains something of the Spirit is called animism. The Amerindians also endow objects in Nature with personal qualities: the river, for example, is called 'the Long Person'. But it is not just the trees, mountains, snow and streams that contain soul, for the animals do so also. This is the belief in the totem beast. The Amerindians might admire and seek to imitate the cunning of the fox, the sensitivity and grace of the deer, the stealth of the wild cat, the wisdom of the owl or the physical strength and resourcefulness of the brown bear. As well as seeing these human characteristics in the animals, the Amerindians also portray the animals in legend as behaving like human beings. Beavers, bears, foxes, fishes and the whole of Nature is blessed with conscious intelligence.

Though such animals were never seen as gods, they were seen as superior in certain ways. The Native Americans gave the animals the very virtues that they wished to develop themselves. For example, there is a story of a modern Amerindian woman's ritual eating of a turtle heart. The turtle is seen to represent the earth, because of its solidity and ability, in its protective shell, to withstand the elements. Also, as it emerges gradually from the water, the turtle is seen to symbolise gestation and growth, and the mountains of old as they are thought to have risen from the sea. This creature represents the slow passage of time, the strength of endurance and stability. The woman had apparently been diagnosed with cancer, and had decided to burn out the disease by applying lighted cigarettes to her body. She swallowed the heart of a turtle in order to give herself the power to cope with the physical pain. As her brother later commented, this animal, 'is about the strongest thing there is. [The heart] keeps on beating for two days after you kill the turtle ... It imparts its power to whoever has eaten of it'.

This demonstrates, in quite a literal way, how the strength

and power of the totem is understood. Individual clans come under the protection of a particular totem animal (the flesh of which they may not eat). After successive generations, tribes came to believe that their particular totem beast was a kind of spiritual ancestor, present also in particular species related to that animal.

The totem beast is also seen in the tradition of the young Amerindian's initiation rite called the vision quest. This takes place at about the age of 15, and involves a fast of four days and nights, in preparation for meeting the totem spirit. The adolescent is sent out alone into the wilderness to find this deity and to listen to its message. In one tale, a boy was sent by his father to seek the spirit of Utonagan, the female ancestral spirit of his tribe. As he climbed the mountain to which he had been sent, he eventually heard the shrill cries of the spirit, which was pursuing him in the guise of a wolf. Overcome with fear, he fled, but his pursuer continued to get closer. Finally, falling to the ground in exhaustion, the boy saw the wolf for what it was, his guardian spirit, who said to him: 'I am she who your family and the Indians call Utonagan. You are dear to me. Look at me, Indian'. He was then no longer afraid, fell into deep slumber and awoke the following day under a bright, sun-drenched sky.

In this example, it's important to stress that the wolf – the totem beast – is seen not as simply a pack animal, but as an indication of the wisdom and intelligence of the Great Spirit. The wolf is one of Nature's various forms, a living expression of this Spirit. By learning about the ways of the animal, we can learn something about the Spirit, too. This differs from the Christian idea of God working in mysterious ways, and the will of man being a separate affair. Native Americans look to God's creatures, including themselves, for clues to the creator. They do not see the totem as having merely symbolic power but believe that it actually embodies that power, be it strength, practical wisdom, or knowledge of the future. Another totem creature, for example, is the eagle, whose ability to soar high up into the clouds, to survey all he sees from a great distance, is associated with the ability (literal and metaphorical) to view the world in a broad, clear-sighted way.

Coyote – The Trickster

Coyote has a prime place in the Amerindian stories. It is important that he is called Coyote rather than 'the Coyote', as this suggests a closeness and familiarity, as occurs in all folk tales. He appears in particular among the tales of the Washoe, Maidu and Chinook, and is an image of the unpredictable wiles of nature. He is sometimes intent on upsetting the

natural order of things, but is usually only involved in minor misbehaviour. For instance, there is the amusing account of how the face of the Bobcat came to be flat. Coyote came upon Bobcat sleeping beneath a tree. He began to sing a magic song so that Bobcat might sleep more soundly. Coyote then began to push against Bobcat's face until it was quite flat. When Bobcat awoke, he saw the new shape of his face in the reflection from a nearby stream. Later Bobcat discovered Coyote asleep. He pulled on Coyote's nose until it stretched, and that is why **Bobcat's face is flat, and Coyote's nose is long.**

This tale demonstrates the Amerindian's sense of humour, but it is important to point out that not all such stories are merely to be lumped under the category of folk tales. Some are stories (probably meant as fiction, as with Bobcat and Coyote) associated with a particular tribe; whilst others are cautionary tales (such as the reminder of why the peace pipe exists). Then, of course, there are the creation myths.

In the Maidu version of the creation of the Amerindian race, Kodoyanpe was the god who first discovered the world with Coyote. Both of them set about making the world a fit place for the human race to live in. They made people from tiny wooden images and when this proved impractical the people were transformed into animals. Kodoyanpe began to suspect that Coyote was delaying the creation of the perfect human and a war broke out as Kodoyanpe tried to overcome Coyote and the monsters who helped him. With the help of a powerful being known as the Conqueror, Kodoyanpe was able to destroy many of Coyote's helpers. He eventually won the war, thanks to some of the older wooden manikins that he had secretly hidden, and which now took their place on earth, in the form of the Amerindian peoples.

This is no simple folk tale. There is the age-old theme of two quarrelling divine beings, one who is good, the other one evil. The evil being tries to stop the good bringing his special creation into the world. There are similarities with the early version of the Greek Prometheus, who made people from clay and water, and taught them medicine, prophecy and healing. Zeus, the king of the gods, later took his revenge on Prometheus, who had also stolen fire from Mount Olympus in order to bring the light of knowledge and wisdom to humans. The story can also be viewed in terms of the eternal struggle between light and dark, day and night. Kodoyanpe is the bright sun, the force for good whose intention is enlightenment, whilst Coyote rules the nocturnal powers that only leave man in darkness. Many of the myths from the near-east have similar duallist theologies, such as the Persian Zarathustra and his dark counterpart Ahriman, or the Egyptian sun god Osiris and his evil brother Set. And yet, it would be inappropriate to try to find Western or Asian versions of the above Native American myth, as Coyote has come down to us without the moral baggage of being evil. But, by the Native Americans themselves, he is considered merely mischievous, a trickster. In fact, in certain Amerindian myths Coyote is kind and good, and sometimes a rather absurd figure. One Winnebago myth in particular tells of how, while skinning a buffalo, Coyote's arms suddenly began fighting with each other, causing him multiple painful cuts. As absurd as this tale sounds, there is a deeper meaning: just when we least expect it, fate can take a turn that defeats all our sense of natural order, our powers of logic and will.

This is the role of the Trickster in mythology. His apparent purpose is to defeat humanity in some way, but his efforts often come unstuck and he suffers just as unpleasant a fate as he had planned for his human victims. In the Blackfoot legends the Trickster figure is Raven, who stole all the game animals – buffalo, deer, antelope – so there would be nothing left to hunt. The creator god, named Old Man, finally discovered the animals in a cave and set them free, but later during a hunt when the Blackfoot tried to drive a buffalo herd over a cliff, the mischievous Raven appeared out of nowhere and drove them back in the opposite direction. Raven was finally punished by the creator god, who suspended him over a fire until he repented and promised to behave in the future. The Trickster, however, is a force of Nature and will not change his ways.

There is a striking parallel between Raven and the cunning Hermes, a trickster figure in classical Greek mythology, who, among other antics, stole cattle from his brother Apollo.

In modern psychology, this idea of fate playing nasty tricks, of being at the mercy of unexpected and maddening obstacles, is connected to an element of the unconscious that Jung called the Shadow. In one sense it is the potential for evil that we all carry, in another, it is our Achilles heel, the energies in the psyche we have not properly embraced. These therefore remain raw, undeveloped or arrested, and we project them on to the world, blaming our bad luck on someone or something else. As Jung says: 'The so-called civilised man has forgotten the trickster. He remembers him only figuratively and metaphorically, when, irritated by his own ineptitude, he speaks of fate playing tricks on him or of things being bewitched.' But it is usually we who have set ourselves up for a fall, often unaware of the consequences of our actions. Even so, our personal life can never be completely under our control, and far from regretting this, Native American tradition acknowledges, even embraces it.

One of the more interesting figures in Algonquian myth is that of Glooskap, whose name means 'the liar'. This name is not an insult but rather a tribute in honour of his wily and cunning nature. In fact, together with his brother Malsum he forms the light half of the good-twin/evil-twin model so common to world mythology. Glooskap created the sun, moon and stars and all the creatures of the earth, including the human race, out of his mother's body as she died giving birth. Malsum (the Trickster), whilst he made the mountains and valleys, set out to create problems for humanity at every step. After having created humans, Glooskap made supernatural entities like elves and fairies and kept two wise birds he would send out into the world to inform him of how his creations were progressing. (This is similar to the Scandinavian myth in which Odin, the ancestor of man, kept two ravens who would fly off each day and then return in their role of eyes and ears of the world.) One day Malsum decided to do away with his own brother. Knowing Glooskap's power over life and death, Malsum asked him if he could ever be killed and how, to which Glooskap replied that death would only come via the touch of an owl's feather. While out hunting, Malsum instructed his friend Wolf to shoot an owl with his bow and arrow and to pluck a feather from the dead creature, then cast it at Glooskap. (Again this reminds us of Loki, the Norse trickster god, responsible for the death of Baldur in a planned accident as the latter was struck with a spear made from mistletoe.) Though Glooskap appeared to be beaten, he immediately rose from the dead. Malsum failed in his attempt and finally came off worse.

What is the purpose of such an unhelpful figure in these tales? I believe the answer lies in a fundamental aspect of human nature, that sometimes the only way in which individuals gain wisdom (about themselves and the world) is through setback and suffering. The easier life is, the more likely you are to become egoistic, without moral purpose or humanity, and with the belief that you are invincible. This point is made clear in the story of Glooskap, whose creation soon began to go wrong. For many years, Glooskap looked after humanity in a kind and gentle manner, killing off just about anything that would threaten the people. He was dismayed to find, however, that though the forces of evil were almost beaten, humankind seemed no better nor wiser; the more he removed potential evil from their lives, the worse they became! Like the spoilt child whose every whim is indulged and who knows neither responsibility nor pain, a detestable monster was being created. Realising his mistake, Glooskap retreated from the world.

Komogwa and Tsonogwa

Generally, in the Amerindian tales there are no good or evil gods. Some evil god in animal form may cause destruction but, unlike, for example, the Christian view, there is no attempt to be rid of the evil. There is no attempt to find the good to the exclusion of the bad. The bad spirits of the forest, or the seas, are to be feared but also respected – we should not simply get rid of them. Nature being random and unpredictable (and evil and disaster do indeed touch the Amerindian) is simply accepted as an occasional fact of life. More than that, as one commentator puts it, 'in many instances, it turns out that what has been reported to be the evil divinity of a nation … is in reality the highest power they recognise'.

The stories of the sea ogre Komogwa and the demon of the forest Tsonogwa illustrate this very un-Western attitude towards destruction as well as a particularly creative way of dealing with it. Among the tribes of the Pacific north-west, the dreaded Komogwa lived beneath the sea. He was bloated and huge, with an insatiable appetite, and his bulbous eyes saw everything. Whenever a Kwakiutl sailor perished in a sea storm, whenever valuable supplies were lost overboard or a fierce-looking whale attacked a canoe, Komogwa was up to his old tricks. On land, the forest was haunted by Tsonogwa, a female ogre with massive pendulous breasts and, with her forever-open mouth and great lips, a never-ending greed. She slyly crept out from her abode to steal young children from their mothers. And yet both of these formidable beings are connected with wealth and the fruits of the earth. (There are similarities here with Pluto, the Roman god of the underworld, whose name means wealth.) Komogwa closely guarded his pile of rich copper, whilst Tsonogwa inhabited a large house in the forest full of material sustenance: fruits, dried meat and animal skins for warmth. The idea is that whilst there are indeed shadowy creatures, even they have something valuable for the Amerindians, if they look for it. Some of the stories about Tsonogwa, for instance, are about the Amerindian returning from the forest in triumph with plentiful goods from her lair. This is not the civilised Western fear of Nature, but an attempt to get the best from it. In putting such a face on Nature – the ogre with a huge store of

great riches – there is an attempt to acknowledge it, to give it some significance. The Native American has made a relationship with the wiles of Nature, accepting and honouring its many facets.

We no longer believe that the gods are angry if it thunders on a stormy night, but to the Amerindian, a merely scientific explanation robs the event of its meaning. We might well look upon animism as belonging to a more primitive age, but maybe the more rational explanations we have, the more we reduce the world to a set of scientific jargon, and the less poetic and magical the world becomes. In any case there are many personal issues, those to do with the inner life of the individual, over which science has no control. These are the issues that arise from the Spirit.

Chapter 3
The Great Unseen

What exactly is meant by Great Spirit, the mysterious author behind all of creation? To some, Spirit is too vague an idea, too ethereal, too far removed from what we can see and touch. The word 'spirit' is also a poor and vague translation of something that is meant to be just as real as physical objects. One authority from the Salish Indians, Wayne Suttles, remarks that 'there is no precise Native equivalent of "Spirit"', and this is because there is no clear boundary between the supernatural and the natural. The Great Unseen is everywhere, in both the material and the spiritual worlds. It may sound paradoxical but there is no real difference between the two: the miraculous and wondrous are simply parts of everyday living.

The Great Spirit, then, is never thought of as some remote god whose ways are totally inexplicable to the Native American, nor has he at one time in the distant past spoken through his prophets so that his teachings may be recorded in a sacred book such as the Bible. The Great Spirit is not there simply to favour the good and punish the wicked, like some impersonal heavenly judge. The relationship between the Native American and Great Spirit is far more intimate. All the

Amerindian has to do is look all around for evidence of Spirit, for as one medicine man puts it, 'civilised people depend too much on man-made printed pages. I turn to the Great Spirit's book which is the whole of creation. You can read a big part of that book if you study nature'. The Great Spirit is the source, and embodiment, of the whole of Nature, which includes the human and animal kingdoms, the world of inanimate objects (whether living, like trees, or not, like rocks) and natural phenomena like night and day, wind and rain, thunder and lightning. But to say merely that the Great Spirit is everything is clearly insufficient. Let's look, then, at some comparisons with other schools of thought.

Taoism and the Way

The ancient Chinese philosophy of Taoism has certain parallels with the way in which the Amerindians see the Great Spirit and the way that it reveals itself. The *Tao Te Ching*, compiled in about the fourth century BC, may be described as a book of personal wisdom which is based upon the changefulness of Nature, and how each thing transforms into its opposite: day into night, heat into cold, movement into stillness. The reality of Nature is therefore change: life never stands still, and we as humans are better off for being 'in the stream'. This principle of change is mirrored in human nature, too: emotionally we move from angry to peaceful and happy to sad, physically from active to inactive. Within each of us lives both the Wise Man and the Fool, the Parent and the Child, the Cynic and the Believer, both masculine and feminine sides. We are never the same thing all of the time, though many of us try to be, to maintain control, forcing ourselves into rigid behaviour patterns, as if there were some fixed self we must live up to. Like the Taoist, the Amerindian recognises and embraces the changefulness and unpredictability of the world, whether in the alternating seasons or in life as a whole. With this attitude, nothing is ever fixed, and there is no attempt to fasten down life, as if it were indeed something that could be controlled. On this facet of Eastern wisdom, author Alan Watts says that it 'has a strictly practical aim, which is not mere knowledge about the Universe; it aims at a transformation of the individual and his feeling for life through experience rather than belief'. The same could be said for the Amerindian in his relationship with the Great Spirit, for it is not a belief in something external, but a close relationship with its presence in everyday life.

This stress on personal experience and self-awareness, on finding a sense of meaning and purpose to life, is central to Native American philosophy. As one Sioux medicine man put it, 'the Great Spirit wants people to be different', but he laments that it is 'only human beings [who] have come to a point where they no longer know why they exist. They have forgotten the secret knowledge of their bodies ... their dreams [which] the spirit has put into every one of them'. All the knowledge and skills required to deal with the practical world, all the instinctual wisdom needed for a happy and balanced life already exist thanks to the Great Spirit. All that is required is to be in tune with it.

To the Amerindian, even the simplest aspects of life that we take for granted are part of the miracle that is Nature. The source of life is therefore not reduced to mere chemical processes, but is the work of Wakan Tanka (the Great Spirit), who provides for the needs of every living creature. According to a Teto Sioux Indian, Okute, Wakan Tanka teaches the birds, plants and animals to carry out their instinctive functions: birds are shown how to make nests, the roots of a plant strive downwards to find more moisture, and everything in Nature knows what to do. This notion of the creator as an all-knowing provider is also found in chapter two of the *Tao Te Ching*: 'myriad creatures rise from it, yet it claims no authority. It gives them life yet claims no possession; It benefits them yet exacts no gratitude.'

Evidence of the Spirit

The Spirit may be described as the life force itself, but it is also what gives us our sense of being: we are not our bodies, our emotions, not even our thoughts, but something beyond this. Spirit is what lies at the heart of the individual. This may sound too simple, but can we accept the alternative – that the whole of human experience is a collection of electro-chemical processes occurring in the brain? Where do our higher qualities that are not dependent on the five senses or brain system come from? Archetypal dreams and longings, the ache for the ideal and the sense that there must be more to life than this may be dismissed as mere fantasy by some, but is that piece of grey-pink matter inside our skull really the sole cause of such wonderment and passion? Likewise, abstract notions such as our sense of justice, individual conscience and our value systems do not come from sense impressions – we already know what is right and good. Here, and in our sense of the poetic, our appreciation of beauty and the workings of Nature, we can detect the Spirit's presence. Without having to move into the realm of the mystic, we may describe the Spirit as a kind of intelligent, organising principle in Nature. There follow some brief examples of the Spirit's presence, which, I hope, will provide an idea of how the Great Spirit is at work in our lives in often unsuspected ways.

Synchronicity

We have all experienced meaningful coincidences in our lives. Carl Jung called these 'an acausal connecting principle'. In terms of Spirit, such occurrences often seem pre-arranged, yet there is often no logical reason for this, apart from a firm sense of rightness that this or that event should happen now. Such events seem to fit so well into the fabric of our lives: the chance encounter, for example, that appears to open the next stage in our progress. As astrologer Liz Greene puts it, such events 'invoke a conviction that another world lies somewhere beneath the apparent one, and intrudes, on suitable occasions, with an experience of fated orderedness'.

Speech

Instead of coming into the world as blank slates who must learn and master various skills, we seem to have some innate knowledge. Spirit, it seems, has already laid out the basic patterns of grammar in speech. This phenomenon may be so subtle that we usually don't bother analysing it; however, it has been shown that, far from children having to learn the rules of sentence formation (getting the nouns, verbs and adjectives in the right order) their ability to form actual statements by themselves already exists. Certainly, young children imitate single words, but – as writer Bill Bryson comments – 'where grammar is concerned, children go their own way'. He sums up: 'In short, children seem to be *programmed* [my italic] to learn language just as they seem to be programmed to learn to walk'.

Science

In the 1940s, scientific breeding experiments on the fruit fly drosophila created an interesting by-product. As the result of a mutant recessive gene, eyeless flies were born. Naturally, the subsequent offspring were eyeless too, but what wasn't to be expected was that after a few generations, the eyes re-appeared. None of this may seem particularly striking, until one realises that it goes against evolutionary theory. What happened with flies simply ought not to have done. To quote science journalist Richard Milton, 'it would be absurd to suggest that nature has repeated [quickly] what is supposed to have taken millions of years'. He goes on to say that 'the fly's genetic mechanism "knows" ... to take effective "action" to compensate'. Of course, science cannot explain what it is that knows the fly ought to possess eyes. There are many other examples like this one, where the result of a scientific experiment shows that some mysterious knowledge is at work. It is why I have described the Spirit as an intelligent principle in Nature, a force that generates and motivates – and is – life itself, a force that might just as well be called the Great Unseen. In the words of Lame Deer: 'The Great Spirit is one, yet he is many'.

Shamanism and the Medicine Man

Most people are familiar with the image of the tribal witch doctor, or shaman, curing a patient's ills by uttering some obscure incantation designed to drive out an evil spirit. In most Northern Asiatic tribes stretching from Finland to Indonesia, the shaman was traditionally a tribal priest who could communicate with native spirits, and use their powers in prophecy and healing. The shaman might use a simple herbal remedy to cure an ill, but would then take on the role of magician in order to locate the spirit that was causing the trouble. In the Native American tradition, shamanic powers are

often passed down the generations, or as occultist Isaac Bonewitz facetiously puts it, 'a shaman was usually a person of unstable mentality who received a "calling", customarily in a dream or vision, and often from some dead shaman who promised to bequeath his powers'.

The Sioux word for medicine man is *wicasa wakan* – holy man. 'Medicine', like many English language renderings of Native American terms, is not a perfect translation of the original word. It certainly refers to more than a bottle of liquid or a box of pills, though one strand of its meaning is perfectly apt, for Native American medicine is whatever is good for you. Therefore, anything that inspires self-knowledge, inner transformation, psychological (and of course physical) well-being and intuitive power, can be termed medicine. Self-understanding and wisdom can also force us to confront the truth about ourselves, which can, of course, be a painful process. Coming face to face with our fears, prejudices and ignorance may be unpleasant, but it is also necessary. Medicine is also about acceptance, discipline, endurance and patience. These same words can be used to describe the vision quest. This is an initiatory trial undergone by the young male Native Americans, who would spend several days alone on a hilltop, with only a blanket and peace pipe. The vision quest is a crucial element in the Amerindian magical tradition, and involves a period of mental and physical endurance in preparation for the vision or voice of the Great Spirit.

Prior to this quest comes the sweat bath, the *inipi,* a purification ritual that always precedes an important ceremony. This purifying rite takes place in a sweat lodge. This is little more than a 1.2-metre (4-foot) high circular hut, but even its construction is symbolic to the Amerindian. 'You start by looking for the right kind of rocks', says the Sioux medicine man Lame Deer, specifically ones bearing apparent 'designs and tracings', which according to tradition have been left there by birds as omens and portents of the future. (Birds have, of course, long been associated with predicting individual futures, weather forecasting and the passage of the soul at death.) Twelve long and supple branches from the willow tree are stripped of bark, and inserted into the ground in a circle. Each branch is bent to the centre and they are all tied together to form a skeletal dome with a square hole at the top. The dome is traditionally covered with buffalo skin. The white branches symbolise continuity with the bones of the tribe's ancestors, whilst the square at the top with its four corners represents the points of the compass, the directions of the wind.

Inside the sweat lodge, a central circular hollow is dug out, in which the stones will later be placed. The earth from the hollow is put outside the hut in a furrowed line. This is a path across which the spirits may enter, and at the end of which is built a small mound, the *unci.* Here, the earth itself is sacred, for it represents the feminine matter from which we are created. The idea is that we are born from the earth and are returned to it in death, or in the more direct words of Lame Deer, 'the earth on which we sit is our grandmother'. The sweat lodge, with its concave circle within another dome-like outer circle, represents the heavens and the earth-circle where we live. The circle is also a symbol of life eternal, the cycle of life and death that is without beginning or end.

The stones that were chosen earlier are then heated in a fire, which signifies the everlasting flame or light of wisdom handed down from the ancestors. Seven naked people enter the sweat lodge counter-clockwise (or east to west, the direction of the setting sun), naturally having to stoop through the low entrance. This is a symbolic act of humility, mirroring the way that animals and insects spend their lives walking and crawling close to the earth. Meanwhile, a helper on the outside brings in the red-hot stones with a forked stick, arranging them in the central hollow. A session of peace-pipe smoking follows, which symbolically unites the participants as brothers and sisters. Finally, in the same way as in a modern sauna, cold water is sprinkled on the rocks. As the steam rises, each participant inhales and imbibes the power of the *inipi,* the breath of the Great Spirit. They then listen for whatever prophecies the stones may utter.

In order for any magical work to take place, those involved need to achieve an altered state of consciousness. Only by going beyond the everyday mind (the usual physical sensations of the body) and removing oneself from the limits of normal

perception, can one contact the Spirit. In the sweat lodge this is achieved through the intense heat of the steam. The Native American shaman has also traditionally used drugs to reach this state, though never simply for recreation. Far from removing oneself from reality in a drug-addled high, these mild hallucinogens are believed to bring the world into sharper focus and significance. This is why certain herbs and plants are considered sacred, and are used to bring about a more vivid kind of awareness wherein the Spirit can speak more audibly. Colours are more vivid, the sensation of time disappears and that feeling of oneness with the universe, of sharing the Spirit, is unmistakable.

Modern physics has shown that the universe is ultimately composed of energy, yet our experiences suggest that there is also an intelligent purpose at work, one of balance and order, that reveals a fundamental unity. And we are part of this! Native American teacher and shaman Jamie Sams puts it thus: 'It's a real different world out there when you can see the energy surrounding every living thing. You see that everything is interconnected. Everything is alive.' She goes on to say that, following the shamanic experience, one comes naturally to a respect for all living things, to realise 'the spark of life that the Creator' has put at our disposal.

Author Kenneth Meadows uses the term shamanics to describe personal self-development through the wisdom of the shaman. He comments, 'the true challenge of our time is to discover our own innermost Self; to uncover who and what we truly are'. So shamanics (or spirit medicine) is about tuning into and developing the gifts from the Spirit. There are comparisons here with depth psychology and Eastern wisdom, as the goal of the shaman is not spiritual perfection, but the realisation and acceptance of who we truly are, of what it is that lives not only within, but without (sometimes referred to as the intelligent, organising principle in Nature). It is the ultimate reality that exists behind the material world, and in the chapter that follows I shall outline the basic stages in the shamanic journey, as plotted on the medicine wheel.

Chapter 4
Squaring the Circle

All Amerindian teachings are based on the holistic attitude towards life: everything is related to everything else, and the substance of the world has its ultimate being in Spirit. The Spirit divides itself up amongst all living things – stones, animals, insects, trees – just as the force from a pebble dropped into a pool radiates outwards into ever widening circles. And as we have seen in the construction of the sweat lodge, the circle within a circle denotes the lesser reflected in the greater, and vice versa. But if the circle symbolises life's eternal cyclic round, it is the square that represents its creations. The square, with its four corners, suggests completeness, totality, a whole, integrated system. In the Native American view, everything truly important in creation comes in a related set of four.

The number four, as with many other magical traditions, possesses great symbolic importance in Amerindian magic. In Sioux medicine, the universe is seen as being composed of four elements: fire, water, earth and air. We speak of the four corners of the universe; there are four compass points with the four directions of the wind. Life is divided into the four kingdoms of human, animal, plant and mineral, and the Sioux

talk of the four virtues a man ought to possess: courage, generosity, endurance and wisdom. Lame Deer points out that 'we do everything by fours: we take four puffs when we smoke the peace pipe ... we pour water four times over the hot rocks in the sweat lodge'. He also suggests that the vision quest lasts for four days and nights in order to honour the four great spirits of the elements: Wakinyan (thunder/fire), Tunkan (stone/earth), Takuskanska (air) and Unktehi (water).

The Medicine Wheel

In Native American philosophy, the four stations of the wind symbolise the four basic vital forces, or elements, of life. They are symbolic totems relating to the seasonal cycle: there is new life, growth and abundance, slow decay and death, and then the renewal of life in the following year. Some might then relate this to the cycle of life, but this pattern of life–death–rebirth can be seen in the human kingdom, and there is no need to believe in past lives to see renewal and rebirth in this life. In this way, the medicine wheel is like the zodiac in modern astrology, whose symbolic beginning is at the first point of spring.

For the Amerindian everything begins and ends in Spirit, so the four winds are yet another expression of the personality of Wakan Tanka. The time of year associated with each wind gets its characteristics from that particular direction. The winds also relate to the fourfold nature of humanity and the related elements: spirit (fire), soul (water), body (earth), and mind (air). These elements may be described in terms of their physical states (fire – energy or radiation; water – liquid; earth – solid and air – gas) or in other areas of teaching they may symbolise the fourfold construction of various systems. In the respective order of fire, water, earth and air, they represent the four faculties of man from ancient Greek philosophy (moral, physical, aesthetic and intellectual); Renaissance Europe's four basic temperaments (choleric, phlegmatic, melancholic and sanguine); the occult planes of experience (etheric, astral, physical and mental) and the four Tarot suits (wands, cups, discs and swords).

The four winds can be represented by a cross with north at the top, positioned within a circle. This symbolises the yearly seasonal cycle from one spring to the next. In Amerindian tradition, the starting place on the circle is the east. This is linked to the rising sun at dawn, or springtime and the emergence of consciousness or birth of Spirit. The springtime winds of the east coincide with Nature coming alive again, and our preparations to venture into the outside world. The sun's apparent daily revolution around the earth is clockwise, which on our wheel takes us next to the south. This fits in with Amerindian thinking that before proceeding into the bright world of daylight and the demands of the outer world (northwards) one must first come to terms with the inner self and its gifts (symbolised by the south). This time of the year, that of the summery south wind, is when the sun is most powerful and Nature is fully alive. It therefore represents a time of growth and blossoming of the Self and of our essential natures. Then, the next station on our clockwise journey is the west, when the autumnal winds are cooler and we must look to our physical circumstances to see what needs to be done. Symbolically, it is a maturation period, a harvest time of gathering in the appropriate resources. Finally, we reach the wintery north winds when Nature seems most inert and restful.

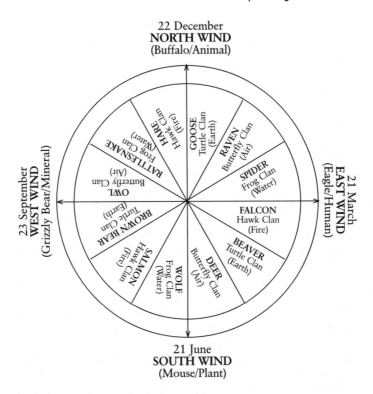

The Spirit Medicine Wheel

The sun is at its weakest in the northern hemisphere at this time of year and this symbolic dying away is a period for renewal and recuperation, but also a time for seeing things in the cold light of day.

Each station of our cross is related to its own totem creature, which is also symbolised by one of the four kingdoms: human, plant, mineral and animal. The four stations are also connected with Jung's system of typology, which states that predominant human types are organised under the headings of intuition, feeling, sensation and thinking. Lastly, each station can be seen as marking the beginning of a new stage of spiritual development. That is, if spring, the time of the east wind, symbolises the dawn of life (in its broadest sense) then each successive season heralds another stage of growth, of consciousness, of human awareness and development until the individual is able to go beyond the human and arrive at the Spirit.

This cycle can be seen in the astrological zodiac, from Aries to Pisces, in which each sign represents different stages or facets of spiritual growth. For example, Capricorn (sign ten) has different lessons to learn than does the first sign, Aries. This does not mean, however, that one is further along the path or more highly evolved than the other. The east wind of spring relates to the first three zodiac signs, what I have called the primitive stage, when the primary lessons of life are learned and we undergo our first stage of development.

A little ought to be said here about the relationship between the symbolic clockwise-moving sun (starting in the east on the wheel) and the four cardinal points throughout the year as they relate to Western astrology. The period for the west wind, for example, begins at the autumnal equinox at around 23 September, an equinoctial point that belongs to the yearly counter-clockwise journey of the sun through the zodiac. The system we are using here depicts the daily clockwise direction of the sun around the earth, which reaches its westerly point at sundown, and corresponds with the annual cardinal point of Libra. As you will see in the correspondences that follow, however, the element associated with the west wind is earth, whilst Libra is an air sign. The idea is not to graft one system perfectly on to the other. However, as far as the elemental scheme goes, the symbolism fits, since if east corresponds with fire, then west – as the opposite point – should be earth since fire characteristics have their opposites in earth, and vice versa. The same applies for air (north) and water (south) – air people are usually everything that water people are not, and vice versa.

The medicine wheel is based on the earth–sun relationship – the 24-hour daily rotation of the earth on its axis – the starting point for which is sunrise in the east. But this cycle is then expressed in a cosmic sense so that sunrise and the east correspond with spring and the vernal equinox, or the first point of Aries. However, in astrology the vernal equinox is graphically represented on the left (the *east* part of the zodiac wheel) with the sun moving counter-clockwise, for this depicts the sun's apparent journey through the zodiac, or the annual rotation of the earth around the sun.

The system of correspondences which follows should be viewed as a scheme representing our general relationship to the rest of life and its cyclic rhythms, or the way in which Great Spirit has gone about his work as architect when constructing the universe.

Winds from the East

Totem

The totem associated with the east wind and its powers is the eagle. Soaring well up above the clouds, apparently reaching to the topmost part of the sky, it has a natural ability to fly close to the realm of Wakan Tanka, Father of the Skies. The flight of the bird is obviously linked with the Spirit realm, and totemic or mythic birds tend to represent the quest to  attain the heights of the mind: awareness and clarity of vision. They are therefore traditionally associated with specialised, intuitive knowledge, a type not gained through the senses but which appears to arrive as if out of thin air. The eagle in flight is an image of a truly open and undivided mind, freed from opinion, emotional judgements, prejudice and from thought itself.

Kingdom

The east wind is associated with the human kingdom, connecting us with the realm of Spirit. Though all living creatures are ultimately one under Wakan Tanka, it is only humankind that has the power of higher perception, and can rise beyond the level of instinct. The power of speech and writing, for example, is a unique gift that allows humans to represent their world in more subtle, sophisticated ways. In ancient Greek and Egyptian thought, this ability to articulate and communicate ideas was a gift from the gods, whose abode was the Spirit realm. The human mind, then, is capable of rising to higher planes of rational thought, moral issues and spiritual values, quite unlike other living beings.

Element

All human nature is a combination of the four elements. In any one individual, though, there will usually be an underlying attitude to life symbolised by one dominant element (or a combination of two). Within the overall personality, a single element is usually strongest, while others seem to play a lesser role, and often a single element is hardly in evidence at all. As the primary element symbolising the spark of life, the east wind is represented by fire. As with astrology, the elements are related to qualities in human nature; we speak of fiery and earthy types, for example. A fiery person may exhibit the same qualities as fire itself. Fire is inconstant, visually dramatic and a source of energy, heat and light, and the same qualities can be seen in fire people who often express a great vivacity, personality and warmth. They are often creative, bright, extroverted types, exuding light with their cheerful spirits. They are usually intuitive, or in other words, enlightened. A powerful symbol for this elemental Spirit can be found in ancient Greek myth of the Titan Prometheus who stole fire from the heavens in order to bring knowledge and illumination to the undeveloped human world.

Jungian Type

The Jungian types are about four different modes of perception. The element of fire is related to the intuitive type that often possesses an uncanny quality of far-vision, and is able to sense an underlying meaning to their lives that other more literal-minded people don't possess. This sense of vision, this ability to sense the future and its impending changes, and being able to see a pattern to life, even borders on the prophetic. But then, their totem bird is also associated with divine knowledge. In Norse mythology, the god Odin transformed himself into an eagle in order to recover one of his stolen treasures – the mead of divine inspiration.

Intention

The east wind is associated with the principle of initiation, with new beginnings, birth and the release of energy into the universe. Certain magical spells require that the practitioner face east when invoking its powers, in order to make the most of its symbolism.

Archetypal Stage

The time period covered by the east wind and its totem, the eagle, relates to the first three signs of the zodiac (spring to summer). This represents the early stage of spiritual development, and stands for awakening, the first stirrings of awareness. The sequence of Aries, Taurus and Gemini takes us from the basic life spirit, or energy (Aries) clothing itself in matter (Taurus) and experiencing the need for the power of movement and consciousness (Gemini).

Winds from the South

Totem

Perhaps not the most prepossessing creature, the totem animal associated with the south wind is the mouse. Its modest size and apparent insignificance are reminders that we humans are, ultimately, equally small and relatively ordinary in the eyes of the Great Spirit. At the same time, its humble size is not the real issue: the mouse is appropriate to this station as it symbolises the art of the small, busily taking care of life's little details, attending to the here and now. As one Native American shaman puts it: 'Mouse analyses and organises, working to bring forth. It helps us to realise we are very small in Grandfather's plan, yet very powerful'. Its totem power is one of sensitivity to environment, and its perspective on life brings it close to things. Unlike the eagle it is unable to see at great distances, but its sensitivity to the things around it is one of its strengths.

Kingdom

The kingdom associated with the south wind is that of the plant. Plants and trees, apart from their obvious ecological benefits in releasing oxygen into the environment, are a powerful expression of Wakan Tanka. Due to their great age and size, certain trees are highly respected by the Amerindian as the containers of ancient wisdom, having both literal and metaphorical qualities of strength and stability. These so-called standing people have for many years provided the means for building homes and the sacred sweat lodge. Then, of course, there is the medicine man's traditional use of particular plants and herbs in healing, aiding perception or emotional balance, or the heightening of the awareness of Spirit. The plant kingdom helps to provide for both physical and spiritual needs. Plants in general, like the humble mouse totem, are extraordinarily sensitive to their surroundings. Apparently, scientific studies have monitored responses from plants to the human voice – and especially to piped music played in the key of C. The stereotyped, humorous image of someone talking gently to their house plant to help it flourish, is less bizarre than it may first appear.

Element

The element belonging to the south wind is water, which is traditionally associated with human feeling. As we travel towards the south on the medicine wheel, we are symbolically

turning inwards, towards the unconscious, the private world of emotion. This is the realm of the human heart, where we respond to others with sensitivity, compassion and empathy. The qualities of actual water are expressed in water people in their ever-shifting and powerful emotions (imagine the eddying currents in a stormy sea) which, restless one day, may be calm the next. Still and undisturbed water has a reflective quality, which means that water people can easily mirror and reflect what comes their way. They sometimes have chameleon-like tendencies, as water assumes the shape of whatever container it happens to be in. This can also express itself as an ability to adapt sensitively to the needs of others. They are the great harmonisers, often having a soothing effect on troubled souls in need of help, and it is in this sense that water is about the giving of nurture and support.

Jungian Type

Related to the south wind and the element of water is Jung's feeling type. Feeling, in this sense, is not mere gut emotion, but rather a kind of sensitivity to the environment, an appreciation for what is right in any given human situation. This type has an ability to establish a sense of balance and proportion in life, not necessarily from decisions based on logic or the emotions, but from whatever it is that ensures harmony. This might sometimes mean going with the flow, but it can mean taking the initiative when necessary, too. Rather like its related mouse totem, the feeling type has a finely tuned sensitivity to atmosphere. Blessed with the ability to make an intuitive reading of any particular human situation, the feeling type has an uncanny sense of what makes others tick, what others are really like beyond the outer personality.

Intention

The principle associated with the south wind is that of giving and nurturing. Just as actual water is something that no living being can do without, so do all of us at times need to express our caring and nurturing instincts. However, the broader principle at work in Amerindian teaching is that all of Great Spirit's creations have something of value to impart to the world, be they material or spiritual properties. What Wakan Tanka has provided for the Amerindian, then, is nothing less than an act of loving support.

Archetypal Stage

The second archetypal stage of awareness relates to Cancer, Leo and Virgo, the period from summer to autumn. I have called this the individual stage, in which human feeling (Cancer) and a sense of uniqueness and importance (Leo) are acquired. These must then be channelled into the practical world (Virgo) to be truly effective. This stage represents the first real awareness of oneself as an individual in one's own right.

Winds from the West

Totem

Symbolically associated with the west wind is the grizzly bear, whose physical resemblance to a rather heavyweight, burly human did not go unnoticed by the Amerindian people of old. In some Native American myths the grizzly is believed to have  walked on two legs, human-like, and to have killed its quarry with a wooden club. This resemblance to human beings is enhanced by the bear's habit, when walking on all fours, of actually using the soles of its feet rather than its toes like other quadrupeds.

The grizzly is famed for its crafty hunting and survival skills; after a huge intake of fruit, nuts and berries during the autumn it lapses into a light sleep (often mistaken for hibernation) during the winter. As a totem the bear has the powers of self-containment, a successful and practical adaptation to the material world as it gathers in resources for future needs (literally or metaphorically). A beast of massive strength and sheer physical power, the bear also symbolises another kind of power, that of pulling through and cleverly outlasting Nature's hostile conditions. This quality meant that the bear was used as a totem in healing rituals among the Blackfoot people. The shaman, wearing the bear's skin and imitating the animal's mannerisms, would paw at the sick person in order to drive away illness.

Kingdom

The kingdom related to the west wind is that of minerals. As ancient manifestations of the physical world, certain rocks and stones are highly revered in Amerindian tradition. We have already encountered the Red Pipe Stone, a gift from the Great Spirit to the Amerindian for use in the smoking of the peace pipe, but crystals, with their various properties, are probably more familiar to us. Their use in modern healing and New Age therapies is now fairly commonplace. The energies of the crystal are in a constant state of electromagnetic balance, enabling them to transform and refine the human energy field. They are ideal for use in Native American medicine, correcting psychological or physical tensions and stresses, and are another reminder that the powers of Wakan Tanka are everywhere.

Element

The element associated with the power of the west is earth, which relates to the physical, material dimension of life. As a symbol for this, actual earth is perfect: it has solidity, stability and the means to support life. On the human level, earth is about the many ways in which we must adapt to the world. No

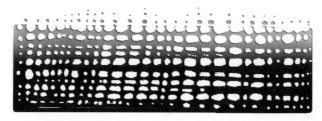

matter how many spiritual or intellectual aspirations we have, we all have to clothe, feed and maintain our bodies. Though this may seem obvious, it contrasts with some traditions that view the body, with its instinctive appetites and desires, as a lower order of reality that needs to be risen above if spiritual perfection is to be achieved. Rather than believing that physical abstinence and suffering on earth equals rewards in a heavenly afterlife, the Amerindian does not separate the higher mind from lower body, but sees the spirit, mind and soul as one. Our body's ability to heal and regulate itself – without our having to think about it – is a little piece of Wakan Tanka's mystery, or what Alan Watts calls the 'wisdom of the body'. Both the body and the world at large have their own set of rules that cannot be broken without causing some kind of suffering. Over-indulgence, lack of sleep or any other kind of abuse of the body will have its effect. The outside world also sets us limitations: no matter how much we may hate growing older and frailer, no matter how quickly we want our desires fulfilled, we still have to make compromises with life. We must therefore attend to the needs of our bodies and of the world around us. As befits the gathering in that takes place in autumn, earth concerns our practical wisdom in acquiring adequate resources, the capacity for work and the patience to see projects through to completion.

Jungian Type

The Jungian type associated with the element of earth is sensation, often described as the reality function. It is the concern with the basic physical reality that we must all deal with. In Jungian psychology, the sensation type is the one best suited to dealing with the material universe and its limitations. This type uses common sense and makes the best of life. It forms a complementary opposite to the fire/intuitive type, for where fire possesses the grand vision, the earth/sensation type has the practical wisdom that makes the most of physical resources.

Intention
Related to the west wind is the function of retaining and holding. At certain times in life it is necessary to sit back and consider one's actions, before moving on. So after the principle of initiation (east wind) in the ripening spring, and provision (south wind) in blossoming summer, comes the need to take stock, to gather in with autumn's holding function.

Archetypal Stage
The west wind represents the social stage in human spiritual development. The primitive stage of growth has brought a sense of individual self, with its own special gifts, values and feelings. The social stage relates to the astrological signs Libra, Scorpio and Sagittarius (autumn to winter). These signs relate to the social, emotional and moral dimensions of life. At this stage the basics of the self are complete and it is the relationships and demands of the outside world that need to be adapted to.

Winds from the North

Totem

The totem beast related to the north wind is the buffalo, the most important animal to the original plains tribes. Dependent upon the buffalo as a source of food, clothing and shelter, the Amerindians went to great lengths to capture it. These included the buffalo dance, in which warriors would wear horned masks, body paint and even tails. Such a dance might last for up to half a day, in imitation of the animal's powerful endurance: the buffalo would often easily outrun its pursuers during a hunt and could survive hot temperatures with very little water. It is therefore a symbol of immense strength; as one Chippewa medicine chief put it, 'the strength of the Buffalo symbolised the strength of the Indians'.

If the west wind represents in-gathering during autumn, the north wind represents nature's long, winter sleep when physical survival is paramount. The mighty buffalo, as provider for the plains tribes, symbolises this survival. In the late nineteenth century, the wanton slaughter of this formidable beast left countless rotting carcasses on the prairie and reduced the number of buffalo from about twenty million to a mere eight hundred. Prior to that, the animal performed a useful ecological function, as grazing herds removed prairie grasses down to the topsoil, enabling herbs and shrubs to sprout. The Native American would naturally have viewed this as an example of instinctual wisdom on the part of Great Spirit: the buffalo knew to do this because Great Spirit had told him to.

Kingdom

Related to the north wind is the animal kingdom and the totemic powers of its inhabitants. The Indian values the innate intelligence of animals, their highly developed sensory awareness, their intuition regarding potential danger and their communicative powers with their own species. Examples of these forms of communication inaudible to the human ear are the low-frequency song of the blue whale, the projected sounds of the Asian elephant and the high-pitched courting noise of the fruit fly. These skills enable the animal to live successfully without the aid of verbal or intellectual powers, and we often take them for granted. The north wind therefore is related to consciousness itself, which furnishes the animal kingdom with its necessary life skills. We have visited the east wind's spirit realm, the south's world of personal feelings and the hardy plane of matter in the west, and now we encounter the experience of mind in the north.

Element

The north wind's related element is air, a traditional symbol for the breath of life, or consciousness. Just as air is invisible, so the soul or spirit that gives life to all sentient beings cannot be seen. If fire rises, earth remains still and water sinks, then air has the power to move horizontally, lightly and invisibly as it swiftly reaches out to make connections with the universe. This is a metaphor for the conscious mind's ability, with its freedom to go where it wishes, to arrive rapidly at answers, judgements and decisions, and to make rational sense of the world. Beneath this is the power of awareness itself and the impressions that appear in our mind, magically, as if out of nowhere.

Placed at the uppermost point on our spirit medicine wheel, the power of the mind symbolically reaches up out of the depths from its opposite position, the intimate emotions of the south. But the north is not concerned with mere ideas and knowledge, rather with the wisdom of experience, and how the lessons we have learned and remembered can best be used.

Jungian Type
Related to the element of air is Jung's thinking type. Like the icy north wind, this type, with its sense of justice and fair play, will often arrive at judgements in a spirit of cold impartiality (the opposite of the feeling world of the hotter south wind). There is an emotionally detached quality about them on a personal level, but this more casual approach usually makes the thinking type a great communicator, with good verbal and mental abilities, and a rapidity of thought and wit often envied by other types. Since the cold north winds are connected to the principle of purification and renewal, so thinking and air symbolise the power of the mind to renew and regenerate. In the wake of some hurtful emotional experience, it is the natural tendency of the mind to begin the healing process. A natural filtering occurs, helping to restore clarity, to infuse new ideas and to provide a clean slate with which to begin life again.

Intention
If the function of the south wind is one of giving, the intention of the north is naturally that of receiving. Our mind appears to receive knowledge, inspiration and ideas as if from some

invisible, mysterious source. Artistic people have likened the mind's ability to tune in and receive creative inspiration to a kind of antenna, which picks up their best ideas almost ready-made. Of course, one need not be an artist to appreciate the mystery of how the correct answer can simply appear when the mind is left to find a solution or to remember something.

Archetypal Stage

The fourth and final archetypal stage, covering the period between winter and the following spring and symbolised by the last three signs of the zodiac, is that of the collective. Having progressed from the social responsibilities and material obligations of the west wind, we now arrive at the pinnacle of achievement in the far north. This involves a much greater integration into society and the rules of life (Capricorn) with our obligations to the social group (Aquarius) and humanity in general (Pisces). Here the individual identity merges with the collective, and realises that it is part of a much greater plan.

Chapter 5
Wheel of Life

W e have seen how the four winds, together with their associated kingdoms and elemental types, form the fourfold basis of the larger, seasonal scheme of things. We may now look at how specific animal totems can symbolise actual birth influences. Below are descriptions of the twelve individual birth totems, a system which could be described as a kind of Amerindian zodiac. Since we are using traditional totems (and not the broader interpretations as with sun signs), these descriptions will tend to focus upon the main aspect of the symbol in question. This is not an attempt to relate each Native American totem to a symbol in the western zodiac, but similarities do occur, and some of the connections with the more familiar zodiac of the ancient Greeks will be pointed out. I have also noted certain mythological correspondences, whether from classical or aboriginal sources. In the same way that a zodiacal sign belongs to one of the four major elements, each totem has a related elemental clan totem. In our first example, the falcon belongs to the hawk clan, in which is embodied the energetic, idealistic and noble spirit of fire.

As with the Western zodiac, the real value of the totems is in what they say about all of us in general. While each relates to a specific type of individual, there is something about these qualities which, to a greater or lesser degree, we all share. As an astrologer friend of mine said of the birth chart, 'you have all of the signs on your chart', and so it is with the totems that follow. Each facet of life symbolised in the Amerindian zodiac has something to teach, and when I refer to the power of a totem, the meaning is again much more than the word 'power' suggests. It is in fact roughly the same as medicine, and therefore power means intelligence, higher instinct, the wisdom to see what is necessary and do it.

The Falcon (21 March – 19 April)

With the falcon, our Amerindian zodiac commences its journey, as we might expect, out of pure Spirit. As one of the princes of the sky, the bird was prized for its ability in hunting, targeting its prey and going swiftly and directly to its target. Its physical characteristics symbolise this skill: the long, powerful claws, the sharp, hooked beak, and those alert and piercing eyes. In many myths, however, the falcon has an even higher quality, as it represents the triumph of Spirit over matter. In Amerindian tradition, the thunderbird had celestial battles with underworld spirits, which were believed to cause earthquakes and frightful storms.

In human life the falcon stands for the freedom of the Spirit, and the need to seek out fresh and exciting challenges in a fearless way. In this energetic, pioneering quality, we can see this totem's relationship to the Western sign of Aries, who is likewise always ready to fight battles for worthy causes. Both symbols are associated with high ideals that are often treated as more important than the real. This is because the forward-looking vision of the falcon is based on elevated principles (such as honesty and loyalty) and optimism for the best of all worlds. But both Aries and the falcon often have unerring judgement and will go straight to their target when the opportunity presents itself.

Elemental Clan Totem: Hawk (Fire)

Generally speaking, fire symbolises the eternal flame of the Spirit, embodied here in the soaring majesty of the falcon. Fire represents the first principle of the universe, the spark of life, the energy without which nothing can live. As a member of the hawk clan then, the falcon symbolises the life force. Like the other birth totems who belong to this clan, falcons can be selfish, and yet the excitement and drama they can bring to others is a direct result of their personal, spirited enthusiasm.

The Beaver (20 April – 20 May)

Perhaps unfamiliar as a birth symbol to the general reader, the beaver holds a special place in Native American tradition. This may be because the animal is so impressive in terms of what it is able to do. A beast of the land, it can also function beneath water for lengthy periods and swim at rapid speeds. For this, Wakan Tanka has provided it with uniquely shaped paws, like paddles,  and an insulating layer of oil within its fur. It also has a wide and flat tail, which it uses as a rudder as it moves through water. The beaver's sharp teeth enable it to saw through branches to make dams. These then create small bodies of water that can be in-filled with earth and twigs to make a home environment.

Beaver people are blessed with practical wisdom and the ability to use resources, whether money or possessions, intelligently and capably. They are the totem of physical security and common-sense wisdom. In the legend of the origin of beaver medicine, the great beaver appears as a wise and benevolent figure, providing shelter and warmth for others. It is chiefly in its role as builder that the beaver relates to the sign of Taurus; both are symbols of the patience and perseverance required to make things happen in the real world. Both contain such qualities as stability, constancy, practicality and the capacity for hard work. As the beaver is an expression of Nature-in-action, so beaver people, like their Taurean relations, are fond of the organic (as opposed to synthetic) world. They have a love of Nature in all its forms, and usually surround themselves with items of the best quality. So the beaver teaches us about the value of the material world.

Elemental Clan Totem: Turtle (Earth)

In the turtle symbol reside the qualities of earth and its solidity. The hard, protective shell represents the power of material survival and endurance, its ponderous speed, the slow passage of time through which imperceptible changes occur in Nature, from the erosion by the sea of pebbles into grains of sand, to the growth of the tallest tree. Whilst the beaver itself can move quickly, its totemic aspect in relation to the turtle clan lies in the whole process of patient building and construction.

The Deer (21 May – 20 June)

The first and most obvious characteristic to note with the deer is its elegant, often wistful beauty, something expressed too in its swift, graceful body movements. Hunters are only too aware of its shyness, its nervous sensitivity regarding intruders, and an alertness that gives it a head start in outrunning pursuers. But among certain shamans, such as those nearby Lake Baikal in Siberia, the deer was connected with the flight of the soul and the acquisition of sacred knowledge. The blood of a freshly killed reindeer was spread over the shaman's ritual tools, as he merged with its spirit during the vision quest. The elusive and agile quality of the deer also symbolises the light touch: that rather playfully detached, casual attitude that likes to learn quickly and then move on.

Deer also need to breathe the air of personal freedom, and like their counterpart in the zodiacal sign of Gemini, their emotions are changeable. One can rarely pin them down on the feeling level, as their natural strength is in the sphere of ideas and intellect. The deer's frequent and nimble movement from one to place to the next symbolises its rapidity of thought, love of variety and change, and ability to see a situation from many angles. On a deeper level the deer represents the very inconstancy of human nature itself, whether our fleeting thoughts or restless, emotional swings. It is for this reason that in Amerindian medicine the totem deer teaches us the value of inner balance, to understand the conflicting opposites within us.

Elemental Clan Totem: Butterfly (Air)

The swift-moving deer belongs to the clan of the butterfly, a winged creature that represents inconstancy, the need for change (literally here as the butterfly changes from caterpillar, to pupa, to its  final stage) and perpetual movement. On a superficial level, this suggests mere curiosity and a love of knowledge for its own sake, but it is also the ability to entertain new ideas without necessarily accepting them as the final truth. Members of the butterfly clan are open, ready to learn and fond of communication in whatever form.

The Wolf (21 June – 21 July)

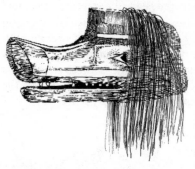

The wolf itself is a formidable, even dangerous, beast, able – through co-operation – to hunt and kill animals several times its own size. The sound of the howling wolf can often prove unsettling to human ears, though in fact these noises are bonding calls to the rest of the pack. Indeed, it is this idea of the pack animal that concerns us: wolves seem to be insecure alone and their family structure resembles that of a tribe, with established leaders and followers. According to Wolf Moondance, the symbol is connected with the 'teacher, pathfinder, protector ... parent'.

In classical myth, the founders of Rome (Romulus and Remus) are nurtured as infants by Lupercal, a massive she-wolf. There are also symbolic connections to the European folklore of the werewolf. Here humans are transformed into werewolves at the full moon, a time associated with madness. This is an exaggerated representation of the inconstant emotional patterns of wolf people who, like the related sign of Cancer, are essentially moon-ruled. Though usually gentle people, wolves, like the seas (whose tides are also influenced by the moon) can prove tempestuous and emotionally stormy when insecure. This totem teaches us the value of personal roots, background and clan as a secure base to fall back on should we need it. Though these needs seem self-evident, and emotional security (wolf) is often graded lower than the powers of thought (deer) in modern culture, the wolf is actually at a further stage of archetypal development than the deer. (See the archetypal stages of the winds in the previous chapter.)

Elemental Clan Totem: Frog (Water)

Water has long been associated with instinct and the feeling world, and the frog, as a shy creature who emerges from water to the land, is a suitable totem. The frog derives its totem power from its transformation from a simple tadpole into a four-legged creature that can inhabit the land. Similarly, the wolf totem is adaptable to different environments and is sensitive to the rhythms of change in nature. The frog clan symbolises the instinctual feelings that connect us to the source of life.

The Salmon (22 July – 21 August)

Salmon are large, migratory freshwater fish that journey into the sea where they mature before returning to their birth-place to spawn. Both impressive and beautiful fish, they can attain lengths of up to 122 cm (4 feet) and can weigh up to 45 kg (100 pounds). The salmon has especially good navigational skills during its migration (possibly using the sun) and its return home is aided by its considerable sense of smell. Due to their success in travelling thousands of miles upstream, often leaping over waterfalls many times their own body length, thence to spawn and die in their millions, the Pacific king salmon embodied strength, courage, purpose and the power of life and death for the north-west coast Indians. Its abundance suggested virility, and its bright rainbow-like colours and connection with solar navigation were links to light, creativity and self-expression.

Like the zodiacal sign of Leo to which they relate, salmon people have a strong desire towards personal expression, to use their innate gifts in an impressive way. In Sioux myth, the salmon is a bold, youthful hero with magical powers. This suggests the Spirit's freedom and ability to transform energy into matter, idea into event, for magic itself is the ultimate creative act. Art, music, writing or any form of creative self-expression allows us to become aware of our unique abilities and to see that we too possess a little of Wakan Tanka's magical power.

Elemental Clan Totem: Hawk (Fire)

The salmon is the second totem belonging to the hawk clan. In both Native American and Celtic myth the fish is linked with foresight and the gifts of the Spirit, or intuitive knowledge. The determination and persistence of the salmon in reaching its objective represents the steady powers of will, differentiating it from the all-encompassing vision and carefree spontaneity of the eagle, the first totem of the hawk clan.

The Brown Bear (22 August – 21 September)

We have already met the bear totem in the previous chapter, and much of what was said there also applies here. The bear is a symbol of physical survival, common sense and wisdom. These qualities are apparent in its preparations for semi-hibernation by gorging on food in order to attain a thick layer of fat. A Blackfoot legend tells of how the boy Sokumapi is helped by bear to survive the cold ravages of winter. Bear teaches the boy a number of techniques, in particular how to transform various unlikely substances into food. Elsewhere in classical myth, there is the belief that bear cubs are born without shape or form, acquiring this only when the mother licks her offspring into shape.

For bear people, this represents their ability to take the raw stuff of the material world and produce tangible results. This can mean either literally making order out of chaos, or subtly organising one's world in a constructive and effective way. Like the sign of Virgo to which they relate, bear people are sensitive to their environment, spending much time analysing and trying to perfect it. Thus, Wolf Moondance describes the bear totem in connection with viewing life 'in an adult way [being] mature about our decisions'. Bears are not only self-reliant in the world at large, they also have an inner order to their whole personality, which prepares them to deal effectively with any life experience.

Elemental Clan Totem: Turtle (Earth)

The second totem belonging to the turtle clan, the bear also has a love of work and organisation. In various ancient myths bears are portrayed as humans who wear their bear coats in the outside world, but remove them indoors to reveal their human identity. This bear coat may be said to symbolise the realistic and common-sense approach necessary to deal with the demands of the outside world. The point is that this coat is worn willingly: bears will work tirelessly in pursuit of dreams, preparing for the day when they sit back, relax and remove their coats.

The Owl (22 September – 22 October)

The owl, traditionally associated with wisdom in world myth, is one of the better known nocturnal birds of prey. Most have large heads, superb hearing, a rather flat face and large, protruding eyes that give excellent binocular vision. Also, its delicate feathers are so fine that it flies virtually without noise. Its status as a bird who flies by night and who thus sees all, added to its unusual ability to turn its head through nearly 180 degrees, is perhaps the reason the owl is connected with prophecy and superior vision. In certain aspects of Native American thinking, the owl was seen as a supernatural guardian; the plains tribes, for example, wore owl feathers as talismans. The owl is the totem bird of the Greek goddess of wisdom, Athene, again a symbol of reason, conscience, fair play and equality.

The owl's ability to use either eye with equal strength is a metaphor for the ability to see both sides to a human situation, and owl people are forever seeking balance in their lives. Like the sign Libra to which they relate, owls have an innate sensitivity to others around them and are at their best in a relationship of one kind or another. Owls teach us the value of rational and impartial judgement, based on the careful weighing of one factor against another.

Elemental Clan Totem: Butterfly (Air)

The second totem belonging to the butterfly clan, owl people use their clear intellect (represented by elemental air) and refined feelings in order to make accurate judgements and to uphold fairness and equality. It is significant that both sexes of owl look very similar, as this symbolises their interest in equality, especially in personal relationships. Like the butterfly, with its perfectly formed symmetrical wings, owl people seek harmony with their 'two sides make a whole' philosophy.

The Rattlesnake (23 October – 22 November)

In legend the world over, the snake is a common symbol of mystery and occult wisdom. Unlike the lofty judgements of the owl, the snake's power resides in its lowly position on the earth, as it slithers along the ground on its belly, in intimate contact with the more base and instinctual side of life. The snake can also appear out of dark, underground spaces where humans cannot go, and thus represents the unconscious and its hidden powers. Whether we see this as emotional insight or secret knowledge of the inner workings of life, snakes often have an intuition that can penetrate to the depths of a situation. In traditional Amerindian teaching the snake is a totem messenger between upper and lower worlds. Their knowledge of the world then does not come from objective facts, but from the depths of the feeling world, where they live for much of the time.

Sensitive in the extreme, they are also highly self-protective. Like the rattlesnake itself, snake people in combat are slow to attack, but once they do, they are extremely venomous. The totem is linked with the sign of Scorpio, with which it shares the ability of periodically shedding its skin, and the theme of death and rebirth. This teaches us the value of transformation and the necessity of giving up whatever has outgrown its use, or no longer supports our psychological growth. This process is often painful, but snakes are attuned to this dying and rebirthing experience out of which arises wisdom and the truth that nothing ever stays the same.

Elemental Clan Totem: Frog (Water)

The second symbol belonging to the frog clan, snake people are deeply emotional, and operate primarily via feelings and intuition. They contain all the innate sensitivities of the frog clan, though these are usually concealed. Just as actual snakes rely on secrecy and stealth, snake people hide their powerful emotions behind a mask of indifference, often because such feelings are difficult to communicate verbally.

The Hare (23 November – 21 December)

The hare is characterised by its alertness and its powerful legs that enable it to outwit pursuers with both great speed and darting changes of direction. Unlike its close relative the rabbit, it prefers to live above the ground in open countryside, and during mating season the males engage in curious bouts of boxing in order to establish superiority. The hare is a bold, boisterous figure who is blessed with speed of thought and quick wits and who needs to breathe the air of freedom. Though relatively humble members of the animal kingdom, hare and rabbit feature as important figures in certain Native American myths. Rabbit, in Sioux legend for example, features as a rash and naïve adventurer, forever getting into scrapes from which he manages to escape. Similarly, Brer Rabbit – African in origin – was a trickster who was able to outwit more powerful figures and to escape death in the nick of time. In one

Amerindian myth, the great hare Manabahzo is a hero who transforms the human race's animal side into something higher, that is, something more elevated, lofty and focused on the spirit.

Like the sign of Sagittarius to which the hare connects, this totem relates to the conflict between Spirit and matter, which is symbolised in the view of human beings as two-legged animals whose spiritual half is forever reaching up towards the realm of the mind. Hare people often have an enlightened, broad view of life, a holistic approach that gives them a sense of meaning and position in the universe. The hare totem teaches us that all things are interconnected: it shows us the all-encompassing, philosophical overview.

Elemental Clan Totem: Hawk (Fire)

In the falcon totem we see the initial outpouring of life energy, and in the salmon its more creative application and a directed sense of purpose. As the third totem belonging to the hawk clan, the hare represents fire in its broader, more social aspect. Hare people, though just as extrovertly spontaneous or selfish as their hawk clan predecessors, are more willing to make compromises with the social order, and their idealism is turned towards higher matters: belief systems, the intellect, philosophy and religion. Their spiritual needs are a little more complex than falcons and salmon: they need to know how everything fits together in a philosophical way.

The Goose (22 December – 19 January)

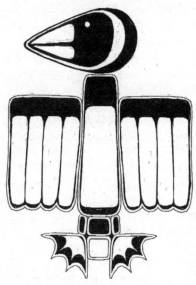

The goose is a large, web-footed and rather bulky water bird that spends much of its time on land. The flight of wild geese, however, often in a familiar 'v' formation, is an impressive sight. These lengthy journeys northward suggest the purifying powers and clarity of mind of the north wind. For the Tungus people of Siberia, the migrating goose is a spirit-helper, transporting the shaman into the otherworld, whilst in Hindu belief it signifies the desire of the soul to be free from its earthly fetters. Both the goose and its related totem the swan are symbols of material power and productivity. Consider the moral tale of the goose able to lay golden eggs and its foolish owners who cut it open expecting to find a store of such eggs inside. The lesson, of course, is that Nature will give up its gifts only slowly to those who are able to understand. Likewise there is the story of the ugly duckling whose unhappy experiences are brought to an end when he realises he is, after all, a beautiful swan. This transformation teaches that life's changes must be accepted and learned from.

Like the related sign of Capricorn, goose people have powerful ambitions towards perfection and excellence. These, however, can only be entirely fulfilled through patience and effort in the real world – just as the goose spends much time on the land. This totem teaches us the value of material experience and learning through hardship, and the lesson that there is no short cut to reward.

Elemental Clan Totem: Turtle (Earth)

We have seen the concern for material security in the beaver and the need to be effective and useful in the brown bear totems. The goose, the third totem of the turtle clan, is distinguished from its predecessors by its powerful aspirations and intense ambition: unlike its related clan totems it is able to leave the ground. The huge distance travelled by the snow goose (up to five thousand miles per year) can be seen as a metaphor for the long-distance (and often difficult) objectives that goose people set themselves. They remain convinced that, no matter how long the journey, they will succeed in finally getting there.

The Raven (20 January – 18 February)

Ravens belong to the crow family of usually large, black-plumed, perching birds. (The crow family also includes the rook, magpie, jay, jackdaw and the more humble starling.) Most of these birds are thieves, attracted to bright objects and stealing eggs from other birds' nests. Whilst traditionally associated with mortality and death in western Europe (due to the habit of scavenging on carrion), the raven's totem power in Amerindian thinking lies in its associations with teaching and knowledge. The Inuit people of Alaska tell of a creation tradition in which the raven originated in the primeval darkness and taught the first humans how to survive. A Haida myth has the raven discovering a giant clam containing small creatures, which it persuades to leave and explore the world beyond. Another legend tells of the raven stealing the sun and bringing gifts of food to mankind. The themes are of a helper of mankind, a concern for the welfare of all, and how knowledge can elevate even the lowliest being. There are similarities with the Greek myth of Prometheus, who stole fire (enlightenment) from heaven for the benefit of the human race.

Like the sign of Aquarius, ravens are progressive (even radical) thinkers with high ideals and fixed principles, and with powerful social ideas of how other people ought to live. On the everyday level they are usually gregarious, loyal and helpful. The raven teaches us the value of brotherhood and charity, that essentially we are all the same, and that what benefits one should benefit all.

Elemental Clan Totem: Butterfly (Air)

The third symbol of the butterfly clan, the intelligent raven represents the powers of reason and thought. The related element of air, which permeates everything, represents strong social inclinations and this is apparent in ravens in their need for many different kinds of relationship. Where the owl is mainly concerned with the one-to-one encounter, raven people thrive in the group situation. The focus of elemental air has progressed from the individual (deer), to the personal relationship (owl) to the social (raven).

The Spider (19 February – 20 March)

Belonging to the arachnid family (along with scorpions, mites and harvestmen), the spider is a small eight-legged carnivore that produces a silken web in which to catch its prey. Prior to mating, spiders undertake an extravagant ritual of visual displays, after which the male often dies from exhaustion. Related to the spider is the harmless false scorpion, the female of which dies as she provides food for her newborn. The symbolism here is of self-sacrifice, the surrender to something greater – a belief system, a higher truth, a charitable cause or simply another individual. Because of their sensitive awareness of the psychic and imaginative realm, spider people don't always feel the need to assert themselves strongly.

The spider's web is also a rich symbol. Like the sign Pisces and the sea it inhabits, the web represents the vastness of creation. In Central America, Ixchel, the Mayan goddess sacred to midwives, assumed the form of a spider, representing Nature itself, the great weaver spinning the thread of life, fate, or possibly, our own nature from which we cannot escape. The web symbolises our fate in that who and what we are is the same as what happens to us. It also represents the interconnectedness (at a spiritual or energy level) of the universe, how everything is ultimately related to everything else and how even the world of form and matter is shifting and changeable. The spider totem therefore teaches us to go beyond our belief that we are separate from life, and to see that everything we do in the world is done to us, whether subtly or obviously.

Elemental Clan Totem: Frog (Water)

The spider is the third and final totem belonging to the frog clan. Like this elemental totem and the second clan symbol, the snake, the spider is one of nature's lowly creatures, close to its instincts and ultra-sensitive to the environment. From the need for emotional security (wolf) we have moved to confrontation with one's own and others' feelings (snake) to arrive at an intuitive understanding of the rhythms and emotional values of life. Though not usually aquatic, there is, in fact, a species of spider that lives in water, craftily constructing a protective, waterproof web above the waterline in which to lay its eggs and hibernate. The ingenious workings of creation take place out of human sight and what is invisible to our physical eyes is often the most powerful: faith, emotion, imagination. Here is a place where the magic happens, the subject of the following chapter.

Chapter 6
Spirit Medicine

The ultimate goal of Native American magic is to manifest the Spirit to its fullest extent. This may however sound meaningless, at least until we know what is actually meant by Spirit. Earlier I described Great Spirit as an intelligent, organising principle in Nature and this definition is the key to what follows, for a part of this principle is contained in the human kingdom. If I further qualified Spirit as our ultimate reality, that life-giving tendency within us, that which desires to live life to the full, we may be nearer to an understanding. Spirit lies, in fact, at the very core of our being.

You may be acquainted with self-help literature in which the subconscious is portrayed as a kind of creative magnet, which we can programme to draw in health, wealth and happiness. I hasten to add that such programming does work (for example with affirmation or visualisation techniques), but have you ever wondered what kind of creative forces are at work here? Supposing a major windfall or unexpected promotion follows your programming of the subconscious. Surely one's mind has not simply reached out and manipulated the universe. Rather, one has tapped into some power, some intelligent, organising principle in the universe. This magical power is not something one possesses, it is something that travels through. We must turn ourselves, to some degree, into a channel for this power.

You may also be familiar with the standard descriptions of the subconscious from the world of psychology: the storehouse of past experience, emotional content, inner drives or the Freudian collection of skeletons and shameful ideas. Whilst psychology's division of the mind into two halves – the solar-like conscious that looks out towards the world and the lunar-like unconscious that looks inwards – may be useful as a guide to the mind, it does seem rather too neat, for what lies at the heart of things is the Spirit. I would say the correct view is not that the Spirit is contained in the subconscious, but that the subconscious is our means of perceiving the Spirit. I believe what ultimately drives us (and the rest of sentient life) is this creative and lifeward force attempting to live through us. The question, 'Why are we here?' can only really be answered by going back to the Spirit.

Neo-Darwinists will tell us that we are at our present human state due to blind chance and random mutations, that humankind is a fortunate accident and that therefore life is fundamentally meaningless. Our notions of meaning and spiritual purpose are therefore self-delusions, and yet it seems that the one thing we resist most fiercely is the suggestion that our lives are valueless. Whether we call it value, meaning or purpose, we have a sense of something higher, beyond our daily lives. We are dimly aware of the spiritual, whether we know it or not. The teachings of traditional Amerindian wisdom are designed to show us that, in fact, we are Spirit beings first and foremost.

I stated earlier that the subconscious mind is essentially the area where Spirit reveals itself, hence dreams and intuition, for example. Our best tool, however, for interpreting the workings of the Spirit is one that the subconscious mind produces spontaneously. It is something that seems to appear at the point between the subconscious and the conscious. It has meaning and emotional importance, and thus lends itself to analysis. It is, of course, the symbol, and the Amerindian's environment is richly symbolic to the point where their meanings are a way of life. As Lame Deer comments, 'we Indians live in a world full of symbols and images where the spiritual and commonplace are one ... To us they are part of nature, part of ourselves – the earth, the sun, the wind and the rain, stones, trees, animals ...'.

The purpose of what follows, then, is to free the conscious mind a little from its strictures. The first step towards Native American teaching is learning to think symbolically, to let the imagination do its work unimpeded. This is not an invitation to indulge in 'anything goes' fantasy, but an opportunity for the mind to use its ability to make associations. It is a serious exercise in looking at how symbolic the world really is.

Making a Spirit Journal

Start by writing down your various impressions, thoughts, feelings and memories on a daily basis. Use a decent-sized notebook and keep it always to hand. Try to free up your imagination and not allow your conscious mind to be distracted by everyday concerns. Your aim is to get in touch with the creative aspects of the Spirit, and the first step will be to see that the imagination is not some peripheral, useless, daydreaming part of ourselves. In order to give yourself a pad on which your imagination can draw, take a walk in the countryside or to the seashore, perhaps to a river bank, or up a lonely hill. Take your Spirit journal with you, and write down the results of your communion. It really does not matter what your initial entries are like, and don't worry about how silly or irrational they are. Spontaneity is all.

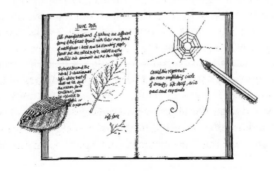

You may find that a major hurdle is a lack of something on which to focus. Visually take in your surroundings and try to absorb the symbolism of whatever is there. You should not need to think too hard about it. Remember that, in Amerindian thinking, all manifestations of Nature are different forms of the Great Spirit with their own types of intelligence: thus trees are standing people; plants are the rooted people; insects are the crawlies and animals are the four-legged. What follows can only be a basic guide, as your own creative mind will be doing the work. The purpose is to get beyond our usual three-dimensional logic, where most of what we see, and the reason for its existence, can be reduced to a scientific or rational explanation. Here are some examples of how you might look at things.

Look closely at the veins of a leaf. Are they not like the veins in our own bodies, distributing the life force? What about the spider's web, is it not a miracle of natural engineering?

Observe carefully the patterns in the grains of certain wooden structures. What do these remind you of? What patterns emerge? Are they like ocean waves or wisps of smoke that keep on changing shape?

Look up into a sky full of clouds. How many different faces are drawn there?

What about the spiral pattern on the shell of the snail? Could this represent an ever-unfolding circle of energy, life itself, as it grows and expands? Remember, the spiral is manifested in ourselves too, in the double-helix of our DNA, the intelligence behind our own forms.

What about the many colours in which Nature appears: what do they represent to you? Which colours are gentle? Which ones are strong? Why is this? Think about it.

These are just brief examples of what you may find in the world around you: feel free to experiment. Colour is one of the most fundamental aspects that we perceive daily and I have listed below a brief summary of traditional colour associations as found in Native American magic. These are often used in both meditations and healing.

Red
The colour of vitality, confidence and passion; the Spirit, energy as the life force from which comes strength and faith in one's abilities.

Orange
The colour of balance, assimilation (combining both red and yellow), a meeting point of Spirit and conscious mind, reminding us of the middle way.

Yellow
The colour of mental creativity, intellectual functions and the mind's ability to conceive, design and envision possible futures.

Green
The colour of growth, harmony, beauty and the physical realm. On a psychological level, growth means learning the lessons of the past so that one may begin again, renewed.

Blue
The colour of truth; the kind of truth that is reached through clarity, depth, emotional understanding and a sincere heart.

Purple
The colour of wisdom; a philosophic and serene wisdom of acceptance, brought about by seeing how the past has led to the present.

Burgundy
The colour of perfection, a combination of confidence (red) and wisdom (purple).

A Shamanic Exercise

The goal of shamanism is to realise how the self is at one with the universe. Before proceeding with this enlightening exercise, let us look at what modern shamans have to say on the subject. Jamie Sams, for instance, comments that the aim of shamanism is a 'total and complete merging [of] your spirit within the whole and finding your place within the whole'. Andy Baggott writes of 'having a close interactive relationship with the whole of creation. And, therefore, whatever you find in creation, that's what you have to align yourself to.' Both commentaries refer to the theme of union, inter-relationship with the whole, an experience that begins in the mind.

Here I present a simple technique for perceiving this uninterrupted wholeness of Spirit and the world around. It is an experience that takes us to the very root of perception itself. It involves no strenuous mental discipline, only a gentle receptivity, although some effort will be involved in avoiding usual thought habits and patterns. Do not expect any miracles of magical transformation, but be aware that the effect can prove wonderfully enlightening.

Before we start, we need to look at how we usually react to the things that we perceive. At each moment during sense perception, as we experience the world either out there or in here, it seems there are words in our head naming what we see, hear and feel, making judgements, reflecting on the past or thinking of possible futures. In this half-conscious process, it is as if we constantly need to remind ourselves of our location in relation to everything else. It is significant that there is always a division into the perceiver (me – subject) and what is perceived (my thoughts, the world – object). The first lesson is that there is no difference whatsoever between you and your thoughts, and the world out there. The apparent difference is created by our mental habits, how we edit our experience, naming, describing, classifying, comparing the objects of perception. The first goal is to get beyond this sense of division. And so, at this point, find a pleasant spot somewhere, preferably outdoors; we are about to look at reality in a rather unusual way.

As I have mentioned, you need no special mental preparation for this exercise in perceiving Spirit, apart from a genuine state of passivity. This may at first prove more difficult than it sounds. Let us say you are looking at a tree in a park; for now this will be your object of perception. In the normal course of events, your mind instantly names the tree, either aloud or in your head. Your mind says 'There is a large oak tree over there'. This happens briefly before your mind moves elsewhere in its incessant chain of thought. What you must now do, perhaps by breaking the chain of thought by first looking away, is to let yourself perceive the tree – its colours, size, its moving branches in the breeze – without thinking. That is, allow yourself to be totally receptive to whatever is around and within at the present moment. You do not need to empty your mind (that, in fact, is not possible), nor try to block out distractions, but to take a gentle watching and waiting attitude.

At first your conscious mind will start to interfere with its internal dialogue, analysing your present reality, dividing up experience into what is seen, felt, heard, thought and so on. You must gently resist this and start again. Your goal is pure openness to the now and its reality, and that means everything you are experiencing. Move your gaze from the tree to whatever else comes into your field of vision. Do not give it a name or consciously think about it. If it is pleasant to look at, just enjoy. Repeat this exercise, but make it effortless. If you are disturbed by noisy traffic in the near distance, let that happen too. You are to absorb everything around you: this is important, for we are concerned with pure experience, with simply what is at the present moment. Again, you will require a little discipline in order to stop thinking, but if you persist with this at-oneness with everything around you, you should begin to experience something unusual.

Perhaps only for a brief moment (though the more you practise this exercise the longer it will last) the barrier between the internal and the external vanishes. The individual doing the perceiving and the external reality merge into one. It is an extraordinary sensation, and the result is an intensity of experience during which you are apt to know intuitively the oneness and wholeness of existence. You sense that your consciousness is creating what is out there, but then, the out there is also in here. You are perceiving via the Spirit. The Spirit, being everywhere, is making its presence felt through you. No conscious analysis is necessary, indeed, the conscious mind, dividing up experience into inner and outer, simply gets in the way. As one Eastern sage put it: '[The Buddhist's] external world and his inner world are for him only two sides of the same fabric, in which the threads of all forces and of all events, of all forms of consciousness and of their objects, are woven into an inseparable net'.

Making a Medicine Wheel

Usually formed from carefully selected stones or rocks, the traditional set-up for the medicine wheel harks back to the commemoration of the buffalo as a totem helper and source of life. In the great outdoors a buffalo skull would be placed at the centre of the wheel to represent the mind of the Great Spirit. By placing stones of various sizes in a four-armed cross inside a circular formation (with an inner circle at the centre), the Amerindians were symbolically representing the great, never-ending wheel of life and its cycles from birth to death and back again. Traditionally, the medicine wheel might use more than 60 stones and would cover an area large enough for the individual to move around inside, making the appropriate symbolic movements from the eastern starting point. What follows is a simpler version, in preparation for contact with the Spirit. The earth medicine wheel bears some similarity to the magician's circle; the difference here is that the Amerindian's wheel is less to do with casting spells, and more to do with establishing inner harmony, self-knowledge and wisdom.

The medicine wheel can be prepared indoors, laid out in a fairly modest size on a plain surface. The actual location is up to you: there is no reason why a wooden table cannot be used. Originally the medicine wheel was laid out on the ground, symbolically to link the Father Spirit to Mother Earth. This is further represented by the cross (matter/Mother) within a circle (spirit/Father). For the symbolic object at the centre of your

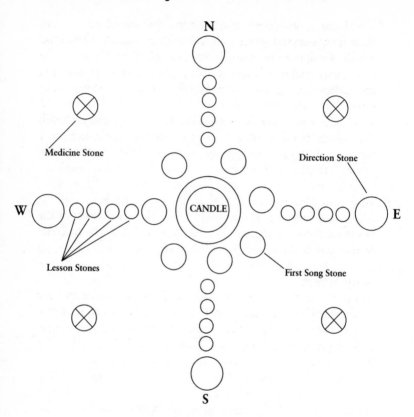

The Earth Medicine Wheel

wheel representing the Spirit, you can either use a large piece of clear quartz crystal (even a crystal ball) or a large, white altar candle. I will use the candle in the example that follows.

You will need four large rocks or pebbles to serve as direction stones; seven medium-sized ones will be your song stones; four more of the same size will be medicine stones, and another 16 small ones will be the lesson stones. All are to be painted with the appropriate colours (enamel paint is preferable and more long-lasting than water-colours) and placed around the wheel in the pattern described below.

Direction Stones

These four largest initial stones stand at the four points of the compass. Place a red stone in the east, blue in the south, green in the west and white in the north.

Song Stones

These seven stones form a circle close to the centre and are placed clockwise starting with a red song stone at a point south-east of the centre. The other six colours are as follows: orange, yellow, green, blue, purple and burgundy.

Lesson Stones

These 16 small stones, divided into four groups of four, form the arms of the cross. For the right horizontal arm in the east, place four small stones painted with a red circle. Place four stones painted with a blue circle to form the vertical pole to the south, then use green for the west and white for the north.

Medicine Stones

Your four remaining stones should be placed equidistant between each of the four compass points, making an outer circle of eight. The first stone should be positioned at south-east, followed by south-west, north-west and finally north-east. The first medicine stone (positioned at south-east) belongs to the east wind and the Spirit, and so you may use your creative imagination when deciding how to paint it. What colours, shapes (regular or otherwise) or symbols, come to mind? If you are artistically gifted you may wish to paint an animal that suggests the power of the Spirit, the east wind, the freedom of the soul, the life force, spiritual energy. Any design will do: it may be stars, planets, fire, birds, even your zodiac sign glyph, for this exercise will begin to show how your creative faculties are operating. You may prefer to do a little quiet meditation first, yet it's largely a matter of just what feels right.

This same exercise should be repeated for the south wind medicine stone (positioned at south-west). This stone represents emotions, so use colours, shapes and forms that speak to you of the realm of the feelings. Continue with the stone for the west wind, representing the body and the material universe, and finally the white stone for the north, symbolising the mind, clarity and purity. Take as little or as much time as you wish with this exercise.

Your earth medicine wheel is now ready for the medicine ritual that follows in the next chapter.

Chapter 7
Spirit Meditations

Now that you have begun to perceive the Spirit, have started to use your Spirit journal and have prepared your own medicine wheel, you are in a position to try some Spirit meditations. These, of course, need to be entered into in a spirit of total sincerity. Your inner self, your subconscious mind, will know whether or not you are committed to medicine workings. You will need to have faith in the Spirit and its possibilities in order for these exercises to work for you.

Purification

Most magical workings require the space in which you are going to operate to be purified. There are different ways of looking at what exactly it is we are attempting to purify. The psychic environment is made up of the vibrations caused by human emotions. During a fierce row these will be particularly strong and need to be cleared away before magic can take place. Traditional occultism speaks of cleansing the aura, the subtle energy field that surrounds the body. There is also the issue of air quality, the atmosphere we breathe, literally and figuratively. Clean, pure air is necessary for good psychological and physical health. Science explains this in terms of the quality of the ions in the air. An ion is an air molecule that can be either negatively or positively charged (according to its electron content) and it is the negative ions that cancel out unnatural pollutants. Whilst domestic devices like ionisers can perform this function, traditional Native American magic would use natural substances like sage, cedarwood or sweet grass, which would be burned to achieve the same effect.

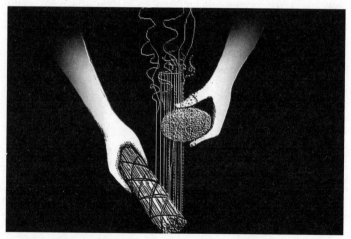

This ceremonial burning is called smudging, and it is customary to use smudging before any kind of shamanic ritual work. You will require therefore a quantity of dried sage or lavender, strung together and burned to produce the purifying smoke. A specially prepared smudge stick can be obtained from New Age supply shops. Alternatively you can use a small quantity of dried sage in a bowl. If you are using this method, light the sage and then extinguish the flame. You may have to keep fanning the sage to ensure that it continues to smoulder. You should then disperse the smoke around the area in which you are going to work. When using the medicine wheel, you should also take each of the medicine stones and pass them through the smoke, before replacing them on the wheel. Once you have performed the smudging ritual, put the stick or bowl to one side and make sure it is no longer smouldering.

Using the Medicine Wheel

Before embarking on any ceremony, you should ensure that you will be free from any external distraction. You may choose to use ear plugs if peripheral noises are likely to disturb you, and you may find that a darkened room is the best place in which to focus on the candle flame at the centre of your medicine wheel. Your mind needs to be in a state of emotional calm so that you can listen to what is within you. Keep your Spirit journal handy so that you can note down any impressions from the ritual, and also have some pieces of paper to hand. Before starting the ceremony, you may want to align the north–south axis of the inner cross on your medicine wheel to actual magnetic north (use a compass to give you the correct bearing). You are then ready to sit in the south before the blue direction stone and light the white altar candle.

Gaze gently at the candle flame: this represents the Spirit, which is also your spirit, the light within. This is symbolically situated at the centre, into which all opposites merge. The colours of the seven song rocks mirror the traditional Amerindian rainbow, whose refracted colours are all produced from the light of the Spirit. You should now follow the steps from the previous chapter that took you to the sense of oneness, whereby you become unaware of yourself as an isolated entity, and what fills you is pure experience. Once you have reached this state, you can then move on to a more formalised part of the ceremony, in which you align your self, the core of your being, with the light produced by the candle.

In your relaxed state, simply observe the flame for as long as it takes to feel the intensity of the experience (again, do not consciously reflect on what you are doing). Sense totally the flame's emotive power, its strength, its warmth. Remember too, that you are not at first attempting to block out anything mentally, but to enter a state of total and utter receptivity: that eternal, illuminating light is you! Once you have achieved this state, you are ready to introduce specific ideas, in a spirit of sincere questioning about your entire existence. You will be seeking answers from the Spirit, and so the ceremony must take the form of a listening approach. This special condition of receptivity is essential if you wish to listen to the Spirit, as this cannot be done on a merely intellectual level.

You should then bring to mind a problem, something to which you are seeking a real answer. It may be some situation in life you feel saddled with. Perhaps your life is not progressing in the way you would wish and you are feeling held back. It could be that you have a definite sense that something is missing in your life. Write down your question on a small piece of paper, and ask the Spirit to provide you with the answer and how you might best take the correct action. Hold the paper over the flame and let it burn. As you do so, give thanks that the problem is already solved. This passing of the problem to the wisdom of the Spirit is a powerfully symbolic action. From this point on you are to forget completely about the issue and trust the Spirit to do its work. Then extinguish the candle, and take it for granted that your answer will be forthcoming, if you have not already received it. Write down any impressions in your Spirit journal and meditate on these.

Though you may find that nothing immediate happens, if you are genuine and sincere in your question, and have faith in the Spirit, you will receive an answer. It may be that the answer you receive is not the one that you wanted, or it may come as a total surprise. Be aware too, that the answer may come at any time, perhaps in a dream or whilst your mind is about other daily business. You may be asked to relinquish certain feelings or attitudes, or you may be asked to take some bold action you would not normally consider.

Elemental Clan Exercises

Though we may say that much Native American magic is about living in harmony with Nature, it fundamentally concerns living in harmony with our own natures. As we have seen, life can be divided into four symbolic elements, the qualities of which we as individuals embody to varying degrees. The following visualisation exercises are a way of both realising our connection to the elements and taking in the powers of each one. Again, the exercises are to be performed in a serious mode, and should be repeated as often as possible. The more work we perform on ourselves, the more in tune we become with the Spirit. But there is a valuable after-effect too, for the general quality of our lives improves as a result.

Your choice of where to carry out these elemental clan exercises may be influenced by the natural orientations of each elemental type. People belonging to the hawk clan (fire) may want to wait for a nice sunny day to perform the fire exercise. Strong hawk types are noticeably at their best in the outdoors, especially absorbing the sun's fiery energy. This is where symbol and literal object meet; the sun is both a physical supporter of life and a powerful totem of the Spirit. Those belonging to the frog clan (water) often find their source of spiritual refreshment in proximity to water, such as rivers, streams, lakes or the sea. Removed from such locations, this type can experience a feeling of spiritual aridity, as if the power of water keeps them connected to the source of life and the richness of their feelings. People of the turtle clan (earth) gain a sense of inner harmony through rapport with the countryside, all forms of greenery and the natural world, whether forests, meadows, trees or rocks. Being too far from Nature can lead these types to feel that life is lacking in substance. Those of the butterfly clan (air) thrive best in the thin, purified air that is found at high altitudes. Obviously, not everyone is within easy travelling distance of the mountains, but as you move higher above sea level, the air becomes more dry and crisp, and even this change can be advantageous.

Whatever your elemental clan according to your birth month, you should perform all of the clan exercises. Remember you are composed of all the elements, though you will usually identify more strongly with one or two specific types. You may perform the meditations in an environment suitable for the chosen clan, or alternatively, you can use your medicine wheel. First you should prepare for the ceremony as above, the only difference being that you will not be using the candle. Instead you should close your eyes and let the remaining visual awareness of the candle become your backdrop.

The visualisations may at first seem quite difficult, especially when you are to imagine yourself without physical form. This is an important step, however, as the ultimate source of life is itself formless. After completing each exercise, and returning to your usual form, jot down any incoming ideas in your Spirit journal. You may be surprised at the amount of insight you achieve. Finally, the ideas that follow are merely short illustrations; you are free, of course, to undertake these journeys unhampered by rules.

Hawk Clan Meditation

This exercise is to be performed sitting outdoors in a comfortable, undisturbed spot, with the sun high in the sky. If you are doing this indoors, visualise the sun and your surrounding environment. Make sure you are in a state of mental calm, and breathe deeply and slowly four times. Here is where your creative imagination can really set to work, for you are about to become the element in question, in this case, fire. First, feel the warmth of the sun on your face, and be aware of nothing else. Then feel the entire solar globe as it encircles you, and you become completely at one with it. You are a radiant sphere of life-energy, giving off endless light, heat and power. Meditate on this. You are a creative force in the universe, since your thoughts attract like situations into your life. At this time your thoughts are full of self-confidence, enthusiasm and faith in the future. Your flames burn brightly and magnificently:

consider this deeply, and think about how your light affects those around you. How do others respond to the real you?

Frog Clan Meditation

Find a quiet, tranquil place beside a body of water: this can be a lake, a river or the sea. First, observe closely the way in which water behaves; see how it reflects the sky and landscape, and wonder at its formlessness. Allow yourself to be drawn under its gentle, potent spell. Sense its power to adapt to whatever shapes in the landscape it contacts, see how it flows along gracefully, without resistance. Water is extremely powerful: it endures and can wear down the largest rock to a tiny grain of sand. You are that actual body of water. You are aware of tremendous, limitless emotional depths within, and whatever comes into contact with you is cleansed and healed, such is your vastness and supreme strength. You enjoy the flow and spontaneity of life; your feelings, and the speed at which they flow, are forever changing, now excitable and rapid, now calm and passive. You are a life-giving element. Meditate on this, and on how the flow of genuine feeling, compassion and tenderness enriches your life and that of your loved ones.

Turtle Clan Meditation

Find a quiet spot where you can be close to trees, such as in a secluded wood or glade. Choose one tree in particular that appeals to you, and sit before it. As an example of earthly matter, the tree is an excellent subject: it possesses a tough, solid aspect that helps it endure all that comes its way, it is strong and silent and appears to stand still, though in fact it is growing, though at an unhurried pace. You are that tree. How does that rock-like solidity and eternal stillness feel? Sense this by seeing the lower part of your body as hard and tough, rooted in the physical earth from which you derive your being. You have an

innate sense of how the material world functions, how things grow and thrive. Should the winds of adversity arrive, part of you remains fixed in the same place, unmoved by the circumstance, whilst the rest of you bends in the breeze, adapting to what must be done. How does this gift of practical intelligence and dependability affect the lives of those around you?

Butterly Clan Meditation

The most appropriate environment for this exercise would be on top of a hill. You should have a sense of altitude and elevation as you look down upon the view below, but the underlying idea is to sense directly the nature and behaviour of

the air – its weightlessness, its purity, its rapidity and swift changes of direction. You may use the image of any small airborne creature, even the butterfly itself, if visualising a body of air proves difficult. First, feel the wind upon your face, then get the feeling of actually being a light, airborne entity as you move with grace and agility around solid objects, pass through tall grasses and up through tree branches, and finally ascend into the skies. How does the view appear from up there? You are in an elevated, detached realm where your speed and height allow you to observe a great deal, with clear, objective vision. And air, like thought, is invisible. Here is one of its powers: as air causes other objects to move, so do certain ideas leave their mark on the human world and can change lives as a result. How does this bird's-eye, see-all perspective on life work for you? How are your ideas able to enlighten those around you?

Living in the Spirit

I call to mind the Power of the World
Which goes round and round and round
Distant sun and far-off skies
In here.

I call to mind the heavenly winds
From East to West and North and South
Their peace and strength, light and warmth
In here.

I call to mind the seasons' round
From icy blast to fertile soil
After the sun there's falling leaves
In here.

I call to mind a sacred Wheel
Its centre where I always stand
A force with the power of One
In here.

I call to mind a Great Mystery
Circular things, without an end
Or beginning or middle
In here.

I call to mind the Great Unseen
For who can say where Spirit starts
And where it goes and if it ends
In here.

I call to mind its eternal Breath
Its wisdom and its strength renewed
Coming back to where it began
In here.

James Lynn Page

Recommended Further Reading

For those wishing to study further the history and teachings of Native American culture and magic, the list below is a reasonably comprehensive guide. I have also included works dealing with mystical traditions from Meso and South America, for they are comparatively similar to the Northern American Indian teachings. Those books marked with an asterisk are particularly recommended.

Alan, Fred, *The Eagle's Quest* (Mandala, 1991)

Andrews, Lynn V., *Teachings Around the Medicine Wheel* (Harper and Row, 1990)

Andrews, Ted, *Animal-speak* (Llewellyn, 1994)

*Bourgault, Luc, *The American Indian Secrets of Crystal Healing* (Foulsham, 1997)

Brown, Dee, *Bury My Heart at Wounded Knee* (Arena, 1987)

*Castaneda, Carlos, *The Teachings of Don Juan: A Yaqui Way of Knowledge* (Penguin Books, 1970); *A Separate Reality* (Penguin Books, 1973); *Journey to Ixtlan* (Penguin Books, 1974); *Tales of Power* (Penguin Books, 1976); *The Second Ring of Power* (Penguin Books, 1979); *The Power of Silence* (Black Swan, 1988)

Chetwynd, Tom, *A Dictionary of Symbols* (Paladin, 1982)

Davidson, Steef (Ed.), *How Can One Sell the Air? The Manifesto of an Indian Chief* (Book Publishing Co.)

*Debo, Angie, *A History of the Indians of the United States* (Pimlico, 1995)

Eliade, Mircea, *Shamanism: Archaic Techniques of Ecstasy* (Princeton University Press, 1976)

Freke, Timothy, *Shamanic Wisdomkeepers* (Godsfield Press, 1999)

Hale, Horatio (Ed.), *Iroquois Book of Rites* (University of Toronto Press, 1963)

Harner, Michael, *The Way of the Shaman* (Bantam Books, 1982)

Kluckhohn, Clyde, *Navajo Witchcraft* (Beacon Press, 1962)

*Lame Deer, *Sioux Medicine Man* (Quartet Books, 1980)

Mails, Thomas E., *The Hopi Survival Guide* (Stewart Tabori & Chang, 1996)

*Meadows, Kenneth, *Earth Medicine: A Shamanic Way to Self Discovery* (Element Books, 1989); *Where Eagles Fly: A Shamanic Way to Inner Wisdom* (Element Books, 1995)

Richardson, James B., *People of the Andes* (Smithsonian Books, 1994)

Rutherford, Ward, *Shamanism – The Foundations of Magic* (Aquarian Press, 1986)

* Saunders, Nicholas, *Animal Spirits* (Macmillan Reference, 1995)

Spence, Lewis, *North American Indians: Myths and Legends* (Senate, 1994)

Steiger, Brad, *Indian Medicine Power* (Para Research, 1984)

Sullivan, William, *The Secrets of the Incas* (Crown, 1996)

Sun Bear, *Buffalo Hearts: A Native American's View of his Culture, Religion and History* (Bear Tribe Publishing, 1976); *At Home in the Wilderness* (Naturegraph Publishers, 1968)

* Sun Bear/Wabun, *The Medicine Wheel* (Prentice Hall, 1980)

Watts, Alan, *The Meaning of Happiness* (Rider, 1978)

Wilcox, Joan Parisi, *Keepers of the Ancient Knowledge: the Mystical World of the Q'ero Indians of Peru* (Element Books, 1999)

* Wolf Moondance, *Rainbow Medicine: a Visionary Guide to Native American Shamanism* (Sterling Publishing, 1994); *Spirit Medicine: Native American Teachings to Awaken the Spirit* (Sterling Publishing, 1995)

Wood, Betty, *The Power of Colour* (Aquarian Press, 1984)

Index